Mississippi River Bend

William Taylor

John Schultz

William Taylor

region*ality*

The Best of Eastern Iowa & Western Illinois

Published by

Quad-City
Times

Mississippi River Bend

O region

ality

Amy Luskey

Larry Fisher

The Best of Eastern Iowa & Western Illinois

Janet Kettelkamp

Publisher
Michael Phelps, Quad-City Times

Executive Project Director
Terry Wilson

Project Directors
Dan Adams
John Humenik
Pat Lee
Debbie McAllister

Writers
Jules Irish, Principal Writer
Jay Crump
David Burke
Abbie Dombrock

Editors
Janet Hill
Jules Irish

Photography Editors
Janet Hill
Jules Irish
Jim Irish
Kristin Keith

Creative Coordinator
Peggy Dykes

Production Director
Janet Hill

Creative Team
Kristin Keith, Principal Designer
Jeanne Ketelaar, Profile Designer
Jo Bowden, Kim Coopman,
Becky Heidgerken, Natalie Pilgrim,
Whitney Smith, Kathy Walsh
and Cindi Worden

Profile Photographers
Leigh Ann Nixon, Principal Photographer
Joe Kelley and Mary Bakeris-Gullion

Digital Color Technician
Tom Heidgerken

Special Project Interns
Anne Kuraitis, Christopher Duke, Kristyn
Verstraete and Sean Gallagher

Cover Photo
Dan Wallace

Back cover photo
Andrew Menees

Cover Design
Eric Tucker

A sincere thank you to the team members of
Northwest Indiana *Oregionality* at *The Times*
of Munster, Ind., for their inspirational idea,
assistance and support in creating Lee
Enterprises' second *Oregionality* book,
Mississippi River Bend – The Best of Eastern
Iowa & Western Illinois.

The Quad-City Times
500 East 3rd Street
Davenport, Iowa 52801

ISBN 1-59152-008-8

Contents

Oregionality

RIGINAL + REGION + PERSONALITY: THIS IS *OREGIONALITY*. A LOOK AT THE BEST OF LIFE IN OUR UNIQUE AREA WHERE THE MIGHTY MISSISSIPPI RIVER RUNS EAST TO WEST. OUR REGION IS RICH WITH IMAGES THAT MAKE US PROUD OF WHO WE ARE AND WHERE WE LIVE. WE HAVE SET ASIDE OUR INHERENT MIDWEST MODESTY FOR THIS CELEBRATION OF OUR VAST SOCIAL AND CULTURAL ADVANTAGES, OUR EXTRAORDINARY NATURAL BEAUTY AND THE HUMAN STRENGTHS THAT SET OUR REGION APART FROM ANYWHERE ELSE IN THE WORLD. THOSE WHO PERUSE ITS PAGES WILL DISCOVER THE DELIGHTFUL JUXTAPOSITIONS THAT OFTEN GO UNKNOWN, OR UNCELEBRATED.

BY JULES IRISH

▲ Greg Boll
▲ John Schultz

This special territory of rich soils, natural wonders and industrious populations that surround the Father of Waters is a place to slow down, settle in and enjoy superior quality of life — a place as close to wholesome as you'll ever find.

With its mixture of small- to medium-sized communities clustered along the banks of the Mississippi River and spreading into the vast farmlands of rural eastern Iowa and western Illinois, it's hard to envision the sum total actually numbers a metropolis-sized 400,000-plus residents. From the beacon city of Davenport, Iowa, to the quiet villages nestled in the countryside, there is much to explore and even more to remember.

It is the river that brought us

here, and it is the river that sustains our presence and growth today. Like John Deere's self-scouring plow that helped tame our region's prairies into fertile farmlands, the U.S. Army Corps of Engineers tamed the roaring river into a navigable waterway with a 29-lock-and-dam system between Minneapolis and St. Louis. Our regional river cities are home to four of these, numbers 13-16.

The region's Mississippi river-front boundaries range in Iowa from Clinton, where one of the widest areas of the upper river measures three miles across, to Muscatine, where we yearn for luscious summer melons and perfect fall pumpkins that burst from the city's sandy river soils. On the Illinois shore, the upper region

extends from Fulton, where an original Dutch windmill is the centerpiece of the town's heritage, downstream to New Boston, where the white pelicans roost and there's no better fishing around. Connecting these boundary towns lie the many bridges that dutifully carry people and goods across the Mississippi and through America's heartland.

The Mighty Miss, Ol' Man River, Great River, no matter what you call it ... the Mississippi River is the Father of Waters and the working and recreational centerpiece of the region. Settlers prized the river and used it almost exclusively to transport goods before the railways, and then highways, came along. Today, barges still gracefully lug commodities such as grain, coal and

Eric Andresen

other natural resources to and from and everywhere in between our Mississippi River's headwaters in Minnesota and its mouth in Louisiana and beyond.

Pushed by powerful towboats that look like they could never bear the burden of the lumbering barges, river freight is a contrast in pace next to the riverfront rail services that transport raw materials and bulk commodities to mainlines throughout North America.

It is also here where the Father of Waters connects with some of its fun-filled offspring. As the Mississippi hustles along, tributaries such as the Rock and Wapsipinicon rivers offer their own lazing attitude toward life on the water.

In between our regional river boundaries lies our nucleus — the Quad-Cities — a misnomer, really, for the 15 or so cities and towns that link together and share the river as a front doorstep. Davenport, population 98,359, and Bettendorf, pop-

Sharon Beckman

ulation 31,275, are the largest Iowa towns in the Quad-Cities. Moline, population 43,768, and Rock Island, population 39,684, take the prize on the Illinois shore.

The Mississippi River Bend Region is the area where the river takes its most dramatic and peculiar twist as the only stretch that runs from east to west, a feature that can confuse those with even the most acute sense of direction.

World travelers stand in awe on the banks of the Mighty Miss, satisfied to fulfill yet another journey on life's to-do lists. In winter, it's the bald eagles; in summer, the great blue herons that compel even the most familiarized Midwesterner to stop and share the spectacle of these giant birds' flights. For those who look close, there's much more to see. Our Mississippi River valley is one of the five major flyways in the U.S.

It is the river, too, that brings us tourism growth. No longer taken for granted, our downtowns are teaming with big-city renaissance that celebrates our great river and farmland heritage. Tourism has taken a front seat in our categories of industry. Our small towns are abundant with activities that

bring to light each community's unique heritage, and antiquing has become a favorite pastime for residents and tourists who ramble our river and country roads.

If you really want to experience the river, our bike paths are the way to travel. On both sides of the river, national and regional trails connect and traverse through myriad towns and natural environments. It is there where you experience the true mystique of river towns and residents who joyfully wave at passersby like they were the first folks they've seen travel through in a week.

For a more intricate look, recreational boating is king. From kayaks on the Wapsipinicon to pontoons on the Rock to sea-worthy yachts on the Mighty Miss, our rivers attract those passionately driven to the water. Riverboat casinos have created their own clever niche in Davenport, Bettendorf and Clinton, Iowa, and in Rock Island, Ill. It's where those who feel lucky, or are just looking for some good food and entertainment, travel from far and wide to experience the action.

We've reinvented the popularity of touring paddle wheelers, too. Day and overnight cruises are grand aboard these renovated

relics of yesteryear at various venues in the region. Even the magnificent Delta Cruise Line brings her big bruisers up our way, stopping to give residents a glimpse of their fantastic glory.

Off shore, our region is the king of corn and soybeans and calls the world's agricultural emperor, John Deere, its very own. This giant's generosity and influence on our past and our present is a point of pride for all who call the area home. Agriculture here also means hogs and cattle, although our innovative farmers are keen to new ideas, and as you cross through the rambling countryside, don't be surprised to see crops such as sunflowers and livestock like ostriches and bison.

The region's position at the crossroads of Middle America has helped it transform into a hub for distribution, manufacturing, food production and transportation. Served by Interstates 74, 80, 88 and 280, the region sets within a day's drive of more than 40 million consumers. The Quad City International Airport, a U.S. Customs Port of Entry, provides one-stop service to virtually anywhere in the world.

Other major advantages include a lower cost of doing business and, of course, our famous hard-working, honest and ethical pool of labor. The area consistently

Mike Leinhauser

ranks as one of the most affordable housing markets in the nation, and the variety of its neighborhoods range from neat and tidy small-town groupings to glorious historic and revitalized river mansions and modern family-friendly suburban living.

In addition to John Deere, the region is home to such manufacturing giants as Alcoa Davenport Works, where its aluminum has contributed to important markets like our nation's space and military programs, and the Rock Island Arsenal, which supports our nation's defense strategy with world-class products and services.

Our quality of life is further accentuated by our educational systems and outstanding health care facilities. With high school graduation rates among the highest in the nation, the region's quality public and parochial education systems are complimented by outstanding private and public colleges and universities.

Whether your sporting or leisure-time interests are quenched from the spectator's seat, flying down a ski run or rappelling from a face of stone carved by the receding waters of the glaciers, opportunities abound. Our AF2 arena football team, UHL professional hockey team and Class A professional baseball team deliver plenty of excitement as their fans cheer them to victory.

More than 900 events are presented annually by our arts and

John Schultz
▼ Kyle-Marie Albert ▲

culture community, which is headlined by our own symphony, professional ballet company, museums, art galleries, and professional and amateur performing art centers.

From the lapping waters of our rivers large and small to the whispering woods of our glorious parks ... from lush fields of corn and soybeans to mammoth manufacturing facilities ... from hometown pageants and parades to world-class urban music festivals ... from pre-schoolers kicking their first soccer balls to high-school and college championship games ... from kindergartners off to their first day of

school to senior citizens learning to line dance ... from inventive industrial machine shops to rollicking riverboat casinos. Farm and factory. Urban and rural. New and old. Roots. Rivers. Resources. Renaissance.

We invite you to join us as we walk among the swaying corn stalks in the richest farmland in the world, as we skip a rock on the only stretch of the longest river in North America that runs east to west, as we carry on a conversation with the hardest-working, most caring, congenial people in the country, and savor some of the most unique characteristics of the Mississippi River Bend region.

Oregionality

Natural Wonders

John Schultz

◄ John Schultz
▼ John Schultz

S undown on the Mississippi shoreline of Ben Butterworth Parkway in Moline – what a great way for mom and daughter to end the day (facing page). Springtime lightning near DeWitt wakes up the Midwest and postpones an Assumption vs. Maquoketa baseball game (top). A cormorant takes flight from the Mississippi River (bottom).

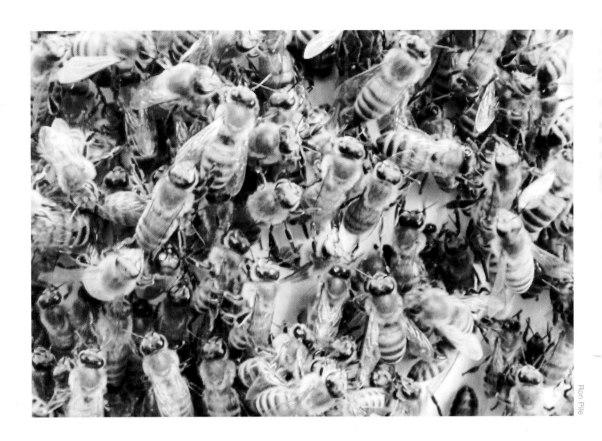

Bees swarm to establish a new hive (top). A blue dasher dragonfly dries his wings in the morning sunlight before hunting for breakfast (bottom). A Monarch butterfly savors the nectar at Thomson-Fulton Sand Prairie (facing page).

Oregionality

Kevin Colby

I cy trees loom on a foggy morning in rural Scott County.

Oregionality

Mississippi River Bend

Oregionality

John Schultz

Jeff Cook

Jurassic Park? No, it's picturesque Wildcat Den State Park in Muscatine (facing page). In the autumn, regional residents hit the blue highways to experience the true beauty of the Midwest's vibrantly colored leaves (top and bottom).

A coopers hawk awaits the arrival of a meal (top). Bald eagles mark the approach of winter in the region's river valleys (bottom).

Oregionality

A family of Canada geese enjoys the serenity of a rural farm pond (top). Another pair watch over their goslings as they learn to maneuver the mighty Mississippi River (bottom).

Diane Dexter-Wall

Lindsey Walters

Bob Motz

Sean Gallagher

A single dew drop battles the sunshine for survival at Blackhawk State Historical Site in Rock Island (top). A busy bee takes a work break on a wildflower (bottom).

Oregionality

Mitzi S. Hook

An ant scales what must seem like a mountain at Thomsen-Fulton Sand Prairie in Fulton (top). A beautiful flower blooms at Bickelhaupt Arboretum in Clinton (bottom).

Marlys Johnson

Nancy L. Purington

Oregionality

An old rotted log makes a great screen for wildlife viewing in LeClaire City Park (facing page top). Water lilies burst from the backwaters of the Mississippi River (facing page bottom). Two newly hatched chicks don't yet realize the world is much bigger than the confines of their cozy nest (top). Hungry babies await the return of their doting mom and dad (bottom).

Two circus cats mix it up between performances at The Mark of the Quad Cities in Moline (top). Circus elephants take pleasure in a cool drink before their next show (bottom).

Greg Boll

Larry Fisher

O r e g i o n a l i t y

Larry Fisher

Shelley Schipper

egional residents regard great blue herons as river royalty (top). You can't help but giggle at the always-entertaining frogs at Davenport's Vander Veer Park lagoon (bottom).

The glory of winter delivers a refreshing new landscape across the region. A weary branch surrenders to the weight of mature pinecones and heavy snowfall (top). Even a simple stick has appeal on freshly fallen snow (bottom). Cardinals fluff their feathers to keep warm on a cold winter day (facing page top left). The last winter snowfall sheds tears at season's end (facing page top right). The uncontested king of the sledding hill enjoys the blissful silence of freshly fallen snow at Longview Park in Rock Island (facing page bottom).

Shirley Dickey

Philip Cunningham

Oregionality

Greg Boll

Theresa Ullrich

Quinn Kirkpatrick

T he moon blots out the sun over the Wells Fargo Bank clock tower in Davenport as North America witnesses a Christmas Day solar eclipse in 2000 – a celestial circumstance that won't happen again until 2307 (facing page). Our regional river backwaters are extraordinary ecosystems teeming with weird and wonderful wildlife.

Greg Boll

Oregionality

Greg Boll

The back yard becomes a natural theater as residents take time to enjoy the antics of the region's bountiful squirrels (facing page top). A majestic buck is keenly aware of this photographer's presence (facing page bottom). When the upper Mississippi freezes over in wintertime, bald eagles migrate south to find open water. Hundreds make this region their winter home as water stays flowing below churning locks and dams. As fish fall down a dam's drop, they are stunned by the force and emerge close to the surface – easy pickings for the big birds of prey.

A field of daisies graces the Syverud property in Pleasant Valley (top). A toddler takes his first steps toward a career at the impressive Deere & Company World Headquarters in Moline (bottom). Visitors to the Bickelhaupt Arboretum in Clinton relax to the calming pulse of a bubbling stream while viewing the center's natural wonders (facing page).

John Schultz

Stephanie Willcox

Oregionality

Mississippi River Bend

An early spring ice storm seals the beauty of developing roses at Vander Veer Park.

T he splendor of a snowfall transforms Moline's Prospect Park into an idyllic winter wonderland.

Fall colors are beautifully reflected across the water at Oakdale Memorial Park in Davenport (top). A statuesque great blue heron stops to ponder his next move while fishing along the Mississippi River in Muscatine (bottom).

Dan Wallace

Beth Hecht

Oregionality

John Schultz

Jeff Cook

A fast moving cold front rumbles across the sky just south of DeWitt (top). Ten times the mass of Halley's Comet, the ominous Hale Bop streaks through the starry night sky in Pleasant Valley (bottom).

Jeff Cook

Kevin Allichin
Jeff Cook

John Schultz

He's found the perfect pumpkin, but how will he get it home? This photo of a concerned pumpkin-picker won fifth place in the *Oregionality* photo contest (facing page). Hundreds enjoy Vietnamese New Year at Sacred Heart Cathedral in Davenport (top). A wide-range of musical talents contribute to the cultural quality of life throughout the region (bottom left). Trapped air and a human pillar make a tent at St. Paul Lutheran Church (bottom right).

Students defy gravity against an endless sky (top). Carefree dancers clad in pioneer clothing have some fun at Heritage Days at Scott County Park (bottom).

John Schultz

Shelley Schipper

Oregionality

Nancy Moler

Day or night, the Mississippi River provides entertainment and relaxation. A small boater strikes a pose in front of the I-280 bridge (top). The sun sets as a walker stops to reflect along the Ben Butterworth Parkway (bottom).

Are you going to eat that? Square dancers take a break for rest and refreshment (top). Between 1846 and 1861, more than 1,000 religious dissenters from Sweden lived at the communal colony, Bishop Hill. Here, acoustic musicians from the Bishop Hill group Just Folks welcome visitors into one of the original restored buildings (bottom). A farm wife shares her secrets for the perfect pie: a flaky crust, fresh strawberries and an antidote for stress (facing page).

Jeff Cook

Greg Boll

Oregionality

Mississippi River Bend

Quad-Citians love to come together for just about anything. Cheerleaders boost team spirit (top left). Volunteers brave the cold to distribute Thanksgiving baskets (top right). Surrounded by fellow fans, teens chat it up while waiting for Britney Spears tickets (bottom).

John Schultz

Larry Fisher

John Schultz

Oregionality

A grandma and baby share a special moment (top). This child's mom was probably a bit startled to turn and see an unfamiliar face (bottom left). A girl holds perfectly still to get her face painted at the Vander Veer Park Fall Festival (bottom right).

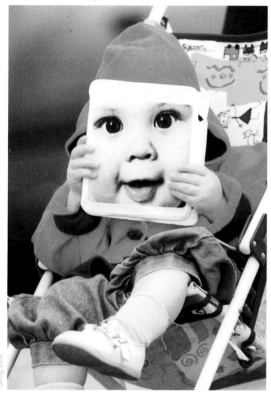

A set of O's: The playground is a great spot to hang out (bottom left). An unsuspecting girl slides into an amiable ambush (bottom right). Everyone's a winner: A Special Olympics participant celebrates (top). At the Martin Luther King Center in Rock Island, Quad-Citians gladly reach out to others, from filling trays with stuffing at the center's annual Thanksgiving meal (facing page top) to passing out gifts at Christmas (facing page bottom).

Oregionality

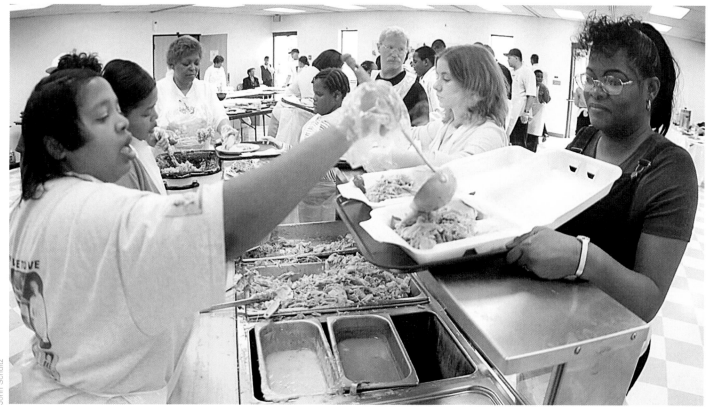

Fast or slow? It's all fun at a father-daughter dance (top). Piglet joins a fast-riding couple during the Toys for Tots motorcycle ride (bottom).

John Schultz

Jeff Cook

Oregionality

Greg Boll

Julie Malake

elebrating freedom of speech: Marquette Street in Davenport commemorates Martin Luther King, Jr. (top). An advocate of peace writes his message in fallen leaves (bottom).

Parked bumper to bumper, buses wait to transport students after a field trip to a Quad-City Youth Symphony concert at the Adler Theater in Davenport.

Oregionality

Jeff Cook

Eric Weber

Jeff Cook

A fence is the perfect peeking height for a boy showing off a lost tooth (top right). An Iowa voter exercises his rights and fulfills his duty (left). Skateboarders test their skills in a Bettendorf neighborhood (bottom right).

Mom, the board is shaking! A swimming instructor encourages an apprehensive diver to take the plunge (top left). Water cascades over friends enjoying a water fountain (top right). This photo of a whooshing waterslide by Quad-City Times photographer, Jeff Cook, was chosen from 15,000 others as the picture of the week on the MSNBC Website (bottom left). Raindrops sparkle as a girl cools off in the spray from a hose (bottom right).

Craig Chandler

Jeff Cook

Jeff Cook

John Schultz

Oregionality

John Schultz

Mississippi River Bend

Racers in the Bettendorf Jaycees Run with Carl memorial run take a moment during the national anthem to remember those who lost their lives Sept. 11, 2001 (top).

Ed Wilson

Melissa Haegele

Oregionality

Deb Rowley

A sunny afternoon provides perfect weather for baseball at Duck Creek Park and fishing at Credit Island (facing page bottom).

tudents receive support from parents, teachers and friends. A mother comforts a new student on her first day of school at Riverdale Heights Elementary in Bettendorf (top). A teacher listens patiently as a pupil asks a question (bottom).

Jeff Cook

Larry Fisher

Oregionality

ands-on activities
teach kids about
the first
Thanksgiving (top). After
school, friends pass the
afternoon at Longview Park
in Rock Island (bottom).

ood plays an important part in entertainment and everyday life. A grill-master contributes to the savory smells at the Bix barbeque (top). A young business owner bonds with her dog while waiting for customers (bottom).

Greg Ball

Larry Fisher

Oregionality

Jeff Cook

Ed Wilson

A Buffalo Bill sighting in LeClaire, the birthplace of William Frederick Cody, a.k.a. Buffalo Bill, in 1846 (top). Rudy Vallejo performs an Eagle Dance in remembrance of our rich American Indian culture at the Quad-Cities Welcome Center in LeClaire, Iowa (bottom).

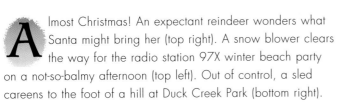

Almost Christmas! An expectant reindeer wonders what Santa might bring her (top right). A snow blower clears the way for the radio station 97X winter beach party on a not-so-balmy afternoon (top left). Out of control, a sled careens to the foot of a hill at Duck Creek Park (bottom right).

Oregionality

F urry friends provide comfort
and companionship.

John Schultz

Volunteering enriches the lives of Quad-Citians donating time at a high school concession stand (top), a senior golf cart tour along the river (middle) and with the United Way (bottom). Huge Legos and friends to share keep day care kids smiling (facing page).

John Schultz

Larry Fisher

Oregionality

John Schultz

Greg Boll

Larry Fisher

Jeff Cook

Events such as the Quad-Cities Criterium see how fast bikers can go on two wheels (facing page). The Quad City International Airport gets travelers on their way throughout the world (top). Rain-soaked streets and highways reflect the busy traffic on the I-74 bridge (bottom left). The Iowa 80 Truck Stop at Walcott, Iowa, claims the title of the world's largest truck stop (bottom right).

Oregionality

Country roads are not far away from the busier traffic in the Quad-Cities (facing page). A bridge span over the Mississippi River provides a panoramic view.

uad-City residents love their automobiles, shined to a high gloss and ready to show off (top and bottom). Many enjoy a variety of auto races at various tracks in the area (facing page top). Being a spectator at a demolition derby can almost be too much to bear (facing page bottom).

Oregionality

Greg Boll

Jeff Cook

Mississippi River Bend

John Schultz

Jeff Cook

T rains provide transportation and enjoyment for many people in the area, whether it be the latest model to come down the track (top) or a classic steam engine that's pulled into Clinton (bottom). A train billows smoke as it rounds a curve (facing page).

Oregionality

rain tracks and bridges provide geometrical variety to the Quad-Cities (top, bottom and facing page top), while different kinds of tracks are made after a Midwest blizzard (facing page bottom).

David DeBlaey

Kevin Colby

Oregionality

Dan Wallace

David Genac

Mississippi River Bend

A Quad-City area bridge provides a panoramic view in the fall (top). Brothers Steven, left, and Patrick Ewald of Taylor Ridge, Ill., wait patiently for the new Whitewater Junction waterpark at Longview Park in Rock Island to open for the day (bottom). Getting out on motorcycles is a favorite activity for many in the Quad-Cities, with several cycle-related events scheduled each year (facing page).

David DeBlaey

Greg Boll

O r e g i o n a l i t y

Craig Chandler

John Schultz

A paddlewheel riverboat provides a link to the past along the Mississippi River (top). Sailing is enjoyable in many seasons — even if you look like Santa Claus (bottom). Interstate 74, which stretches to Cincinnati, has its start in Bettendorf (facing page top). The Quad-Cities is almost the midway point of Interstate 80, which runs from San Francisco to Teaneck, N.J. (facing page bottom).

Oregionality

Dustin Roelle

Many take extra pride in making their cars look as slick and new as the day they came off the assembly line, even if it was 50 years ago. The care of a shine on a car is evidence of the owner's pride (facing page).

Mississippi River Bend

hird Street in Davenport is lighted up for drivers and pedestrians (top). A drawspan over the Government Bridge swings open for passing boat traffic (bottom). A tugboat makes its way up the Mississippi River (facing page).

Don Richhart III

Mississippi River Bend

T he traditional Ride the River, sponsored by River Action, brings families together every Father's Day. The Celebration Belle provides entertainment, food and a ride along the river on a paddleboat (facing page).

Oregionality

Mississippi River Bend

akeoffs and landings are a frequent site at the Quad City International Airport (top). Customers line up at the airport's AirTran counter (bottom). An AirTran plane prepares for take off (facing page top). A smaller plane makes a river landing on the Rock River (facing page bottom).

Oregionality

Greg Boll

Jane E. Mockmore

John Schultz

▲ Greg Boll
▼ Greg Boll

The faces of faith are many in the Mississippi River Bend Region. Nowhere was it more apparent than when citizens gathered in LeClaire Park in Davenport to pray for victims of the Sept. 11, 2001, terrorist attacks (facing page). Young people create their own modern worship traditions (top). Congregations take great pride in preserving the many stunning architectural features of their houses of worship (bottom).

Jeff Cook

John Schultz

F or many, spirituality is the foundation of family and community life (left). Michele Ford raises her hand in prayer during services at the Greater Antioch Baptist Church for victims of terrorism (right).

Oregionality

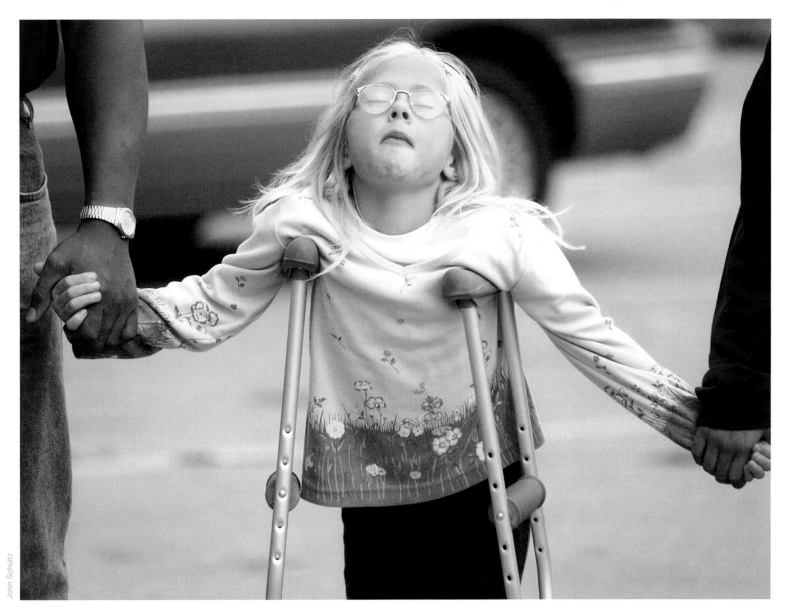

H ope Karwoski supports herself with the help of her crutches and two friends during a prayer in the schools event.

Christians take part in the Walk of the Cross on Good Friday (left). Young girls lead the procession at an area church (right). Holocaust survivor Leon Celnik lights one of the nine candles for Holocaust victims during a Yom Hashoah remembrance ceremony (facing page).

Oregionality

Let there be light: A worshiper and a worker are silhouetted in the light of beautiful church stained glass. This Nativity scene window of St. Pius X Catholic Church in Rock Island was built so well that it actually helps hold up the building (facing page).

Amy Luskey

Dan Wallace

Religious buildings of breathtaking beauty that abound across the region include St. Boniface Church in Clinton, Iowa (left) and St. Paul's Catholic Church in Davenport (right).

Oregionality

ountry churches range from simple to elegant. Country churches have served the region well. Some are just a memory now, including this structure (top). This St. Donatus church is a striking structure amidst surrounding farm fields and forests (bottom).

B onnie Cashen, left, and Ora Mae Lampkin, right, sing "America the Beautiful" during opening night of a four-day crusade at The Mark of the Quad-Cities.

Oregionality

Greg Boll

John Schultz

 musician creates music for the soul, from his soul (left). Rosalind Kirk, left, and Valerie Davis harmonize during gospel choir practice at the Third Mississippi Baptist Church, Davenport (right).

Bishop of Quincy, the Right Rev. Keith Ackerman, SCC, D.D., bestows a prayer upon the Rev. Douglas Grandon during ordination ceremonies at the Christ Episcopal Church in Moline.

John Schultz

Oregionality

Greg Boll

Sean Gallagher

Father Michael Driscoll of St. Mary's Catholic Church in Rock Island prepares for an upcoming Latin service (top). Rev. Rob Lathrop raises the chalice before communion at St. Alphonsus Church in Davenport (bottom).

Children, the bright lights of the future, learn to express their faith through lessons and love (top and bottom and facing page top). Students at St. Paul The Apostle School in Davenport bid farewell to a favorite priest who takes leave to serve as chaplain for the troops in Iraq (facing page bottom).

Oregionality

Jeff Cook

Larry Fisher

Mississippi River Bend

Members of Messiahs Temple Apostolic Faith Church in Davenport congregate for a post dedication service commemorating more than 20 years of building improvements (top). Farzana Kanwar, left, Afsana Abdullah and her daughter, Rebecca, celebrate the end of Ramadan at the Muslim Center of the Quad-Cities (bottom).

Oregionality

inisters discuss plans for the Jerusalem Temple Apostolic Church in Davenport (top). Church trustee Bob Bolte pulls shades over stained glass windows at the Baptist Church in Camanche, Iowa (bottom).

Greg Boll

Volunteer Salvation Army bell ringer Jerry Roskens mans his station in front of K&K Hardware in Bettendorf.

Oregionality

H undreds of people participate in the annual Crop Walk throughout the Quad-Cities, trekking from Memorial Christian Church in Rock Island, through the District of Rock Island, across the Centennial Bridge and through the streets of Davenport.

M ary Ann Schaecher reads the Bible during her prayer hour at St. Pius X chapel in Rock Island (top). Parishioners begin to gather for services at Mt. Zion Community Church on Campbell's Island (bottom).

Oregionality

John Schultz

At an interfaith event at Vander Veer Park, held to remember the terrorist attacks of Sept. 11, 2001, six-year-old Mariah Orr of Rock Island solemnly listens.

On The Farm

Jeff Cook

Jeff Cook

◄ Jeff Cook
▼ Jeff Cook

Jeff Cook

F armers are fond of the freedoms our flags represent and fly them proudly as they toil in their fields (facing page). Worth the waiting – Iowa and Illinois soybeans and corn help to feed the world (top and bottom right). On farms across the region, the old red rooster still serves as the faithful morning alarm clock (bottom left).

F ollowed by a cloud of dust, a farmer harvests soybeans on a rolling field (top). An old farm is weathered into nature as time takes its course in Pleasant Valley (bottom).

Oregionality

 orn country: The crop lies in rows ready for harvest.

R emnants of the past dot the farms and fields of America's Heartland. This photo of the sun setting on an empty corn silo by Jack Greer is the grand-prize winner of the *Oregionality* photo contest.

Jack Greer

Mississippi River Bend   119

Dawn Demler

Rachelle Schneider

Sherry Reicks

Oregionality

Rachelle Schneider

here's nothing like growing up on a farm. Kids find a friend at Vir-Jo Farm in Muscatine (facing page top left), play with a tiny tractor (facing page top right), sustain life (facing page bottom), glory in a bountiful garden in Muscatine (top) and pose for a picture with a cloven-hoofed family member (bottom).

Amy Luskey

nimals give the farm character. Pigs share a tidbit of juicy gossip (top). Sheep contentedly chomp alfalfa (bottom).

Oregionality

Angela Whitmore

Rebecca L. Kauffman

Who says animals don't talk? A horse at Bentley Farm snickers (top left). Tuckered out, horses rest on the ground at Walker Stables in Princeton (top right and bottom).

Rebecca L. Kauffman

 orse whisperer: A friendly pupil nuzzles its trainer during a lesson.

Oregionality

 ld farm equipment is still in high demand, as evidenced by an antique tractor show in the Village of East Davenport.

A farm lane serves as a runway for a recently departed visitor (top). Ice encases wicked-looking barbed wire (bottom).

Polly DeBlaey

Philip Cunningham

Oregionality

An old oak stretches its branches in an open field.

A curious farm dog is rewarded with a frozen nose (top). A farmhouse and buildings lie nestled in the snow at Hamilton's Lost Creek Farm in Princeton (bottom).

Oregionality

F lower gardens and crops thrive (top) as an old tractor evokes nostalgia (bottom) on a farm near Blue Grass, Iowa.

T he setting sun peeks from behind a gambrel-roofed barn (top). Weathered hands twist straw into a broom (bottom).

Oregionalit

This dramatic shot of geese over a farm field at sundown won fourth place in the *Oregionality* photo contest (top). A smart farmer invites friends to celebrate antique tractors and gets his field plowed (bottom).

ANTIQUE PLOWING APRIL 29

A windmill catches the breeze, interrupting the bright sky in Camanche (top). A rainbow promises better years to come (bottom).

Oregionality

Rachelle Schneider

A sunflower basks in the sunshine (top). Nothing runs like a Deere: A restored 2-cylinder tractor is still looking good after all these years (bottom).

Janet Hossmiller-Miller

Jeff Cook

Jeff Cook

Craig Chandler

Oregionality

Another harvest nears its close: Soybeans ripen (facing page top left and right) and are harvested (facing page bottom). From the air, art and science converge, creating a patchwork pattern across our vast farm fields.

John Schultz

T he fields are readied for another year (top). Soybeans are put into storage bins (bottom).

Oregionality

Angela Whitmore

Philip Cunningham

A new puppy explores freshly fallen snow and its owner's shoelaces (top). This indestructible steel exists to plant and harvest the temporal corn (bottom).

Mississippi River Bend

O f farm and family: A close-knit twosome behold their beloved country paradise (top). Another year gone – farmers hustle to harvest at the season's high point (bottom).

Oregionality

The morning sun breaks over a farm on Utica Ridge Road in Davenport (top). The faces of our region's farmers – wholesome, hardy, happy (bottom left and right).

Craig Chandler

Craig Chandler

Oregionality

Jeff Cook

Jeff Cook

Jeff Cook

G ood money, good tan – teens are traditionally tapped for corn de-tasseling (facing page top). A little help from the friendly neighborhood crop duster ensures a bountiful harvest (facing page bottom). Ready for picking, field corn keeps our farm animals healthy (top left and bottom). Rural farmers take pride in keeping their equipment in tip-top running condition, even if it does need a new paint job (top right).

Mississippi River Bend

Hearts and Minds

John Schultz

Greg Boll ▲
Sean Gallagher ▼

The Mark of the Quad Cities in Moline has delivered big-city cultural opportunities to the region, including a stellar performance by guitar virtuoso Eric Clapton (facing page). A Ballet Folklorico dancer twirls through her routine at the Viva Quad Cities festival on Moline's John Deere Commons (top). A young actress prepares for her role in a theater performance at the highly popular Circa 21 Dinner Playhouse in Rock Island (bottom).

Cellist Estelle Miller entertains holiday visitors at First Congregational Church in Geneseo during the town's annual Victorian Christmas Walk.

Oregionality

onductor Ronald Schleicher leads the Quad City Symphony Orchestra in its annual season opener, the Riverfront Pops Concert, in Davenport's LeClaire Park (top). The 2002 Riverfront Pops played to a packed-park crowd, featured visiting tuba virtuoso Patrick Sheridan (bottom) and ended with the event's traditional finale, Tchaikovsky's "1812 Overture," complete with cannon fire and fireworks.

The bishop statue at St. Ambrose University stands guard over students at this private college in the heart of Davenport (top). St. Ambrose, founded in 1882 as a seminary and school of commerce for young men, is now a co-educational university. Ambrose Hall was the first campus building, built in 1885 (bottom).

Oregionality

T he Children's Sculpture Garden in Davenport's Vander Veer Park features life-sized figures of children playing amid the surrounding flowers.

Jeff Cook

B allet Quad Cities dancer Iona Newell, left, demonstrates the finer points of her art during a presentation to children at the Deere-Wiman House in Moline. Mom worries about form as little Maggie tries to stand on her tippy toes (facing page left). A young ballerina delivers all she's got at her first recital (facing page right).

Jeff Cook

Greg Boll

An earth ball provides a whole new atmosphere for learning geography (top). High school students test stream water quality near Walcott during this science outing (bottom).

Oregionality

A Pleasant Valley High School student lends her creative skills to paint a school mural (top). At Bettendorf High School, a different style of painting reminds a visiting wrestling squad that the Bulldogs are the top dogs here (bottom).

The Quad City Arts Festival of Trees is one of the five largest events of its kind in North America. This spectacular nine-night/10-day event at Davenport's RiverCenter/Adler Theatre ushers in the holiday season, attracts more than 80,000 people and annually raises more than $2 million to support local arts and humanities programs in the Quad-Cities (top, bottom and facing page).

Oregionality

Blues are big in the Quad-Cities thanks to the Mississippi Valley Blues Society, which works hard to enhance appreciation and understanding of blues-related music. From regional favorites like Harmonica Slim, playing here with the Pena Brothers at Bent River Brewing Company in Moline (top), to big-time heroes like B.B. King playing at the Adler Theatre in Davenport (facing page), the blues are alive and kicking across the region. Becoming a professional musician starts with lots of practice. High school band members get to school early and stay late to perfect their potential vocation (bottom).

Oregionality

John Schultz

igh school show choirs sing their hearts out during an invitational competition at the RiverCenter/Adler Theatre in Davenport (top). The annual Christmas Walk in the Village of East Davenport presents a fascinating array of living windows, including elves glazing sculptures in the Isabel Bloom workshop (bottom).

O r e g i o n a l i t y

R ev. James Marchionda toots his horn during rehearsal with the New Spirit Singers, a choir created by the Catholic parishes in the Illinois Quad-Cities (top). Salvation Army Major James Fry, bottom right, is a guest singer at the Men's Rehabilitation Center Christmas concert (bottom).

Our region is teeming with a variety of highly talented dance troops (top). An aspiring musician listens intently as she receives a flute lesson (facing page top). A new exhibit is prepared for public display at the Davenport Museum of Art (facing page bottom).

Oregionality

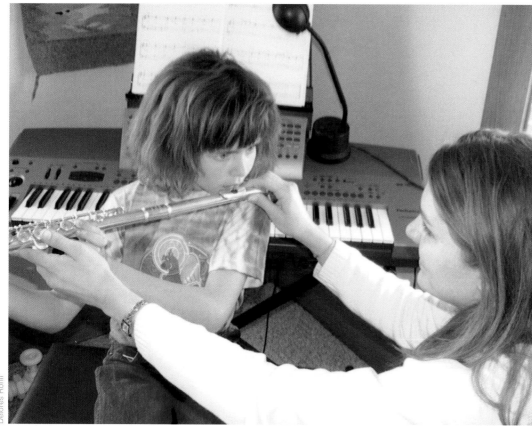

Mississippi River Bend

John Schultz

Quality regional libraries, including the Bettendorf Public Library, play essential roles in developing minds and enhancing quality of life. Clever graduates from our area colleges deliver their heartfelt appreciation for the opportunity to achieve (facing page left). John Deere Middle School in Moline is representative of the regional school system's attention to quality in learning (facing page right).

Oregionality

John Schultz

Kathy Finley

Kids from all over the region, including this funny face aboard a school bus, travel to Davenport for Symphony Day at the Adler Theatre, a live concert by the Quad City Youth Symphony Orchestra (top). A St. Ambrose University student studies hard at the school's handsome and high-tech O'Keefe Library (bottom).

O r e g i o n a l i t y

Jeff Cook

Greg Boll

A young student gives our photographer her best pout as she waits for class to begin at Rock Island's Morning Star Academy (top). Bettendorf High School students never fail to have fun while participating in the Quad City Student Hunger Drive, a friendly competition between 14 area schools that annually contributes hundreds of thousands of pounds of food for the River Bend Food Bank (bottom).

Oregionality

Glass Impact in Rock Island brings the art of glass blowing to the forefront of the region's cultural experiences (facing page top). Twice a year, highly talented juried artists sell their work to enthusiastic crowds at Davenport's Beaux Arts Fair (facing page bottom). If it weren't for volunteers, a lot of regional initiatives would not be possible. Here, Elizabeth Thompson and her brother Tom work hard assisting Habitat for Humanity volunteers build Elizabeth's new home in Moline (top). Volunteers Elaine Benauer, left, and Kelly Grubbs work the T-shirt table to raise funds for a new concession stand (bottom).

I t's a regional family tradition to visit Davenport's historic Vander Veer Park Conservatory as changing flowering exhibits highlight the season of the moment.

Oregionality

Larry Fisher

At Davenport's Vander Veer Park, the Majestic Hope statue by local artist Tom Gleich brings new life to an old, damaged sycamore tree (top). At Davenport's Credit Island Park, these life-sized figures, carved by local artist Tom Gleich and painted with the help of Davenport Central High School students, mimic the George Seurat painting titled "Sunday Afternoon on the Isle of La Grand Jatte" (bottom).

Shirley Dickey

Rivers & Waterways

Greg Boll

John Schultz ▲
▼ Mary Lucas

T his aerial view showcases our region's mighty Mississippi River, including the Centennial Bridge, which is known for its unique architecture and aesthetic appeal (facing page). Nationally known river activist Chad Pregracke, founder of Living Lands & Waters, is one of our region's own (top). This serene shot of the Davenport LeClaire Park Riverfront won second place in the *Oregionality* photo contest (bottom).

Anthony O'Leary

Greg Boll

White pelicans flock at Lock & Dam 16 along the Mississippi in Muscatine (top). Ducks take flight in a snowy winter morning mist (bottom).

Craig Chandler

Jeff Cook

 ids learn a lesson and have fun with frogs at Davenport's Nahant Marsh (top).
Having fun, fun, fun with mama during an outing on the Mississippi River (bottom).

V isitors receive a unique education on the Mississippi River Lock & Dam system at riverfront Leach Park in Bettendorf (top). Persistent anglers enjoy a sunny winter day fishing for walleye at Davenport's Lock & Dam 15 (bottom).

John Schultz

Larry Fisher

Oregionality

Jeff Cook

This barge cleat and mooring line reveal the river's power (top). A solitary fishing spot – the best kind – in Clinton (bottom).

Larry Fisher

Mississippi River Bend

Oregionality

Every season reveals new natural beauty at Crow Creek Park in Bettendorf (facing page). A barge awaits another strenuous journey at Lock & Dam 14 in LeClaire.

Lindsey Walters

The open waters below our region's Mississippi River lock and dam system attract hundreds of wintering bald eagles (top). A mature bald eagle and a young offspring jockey for ice-flow rights (bottom).

Oregionality

B arges are vessels filled with
many visually interesting features.

A grand view from Rock Island to Davenport of the Mississippi's Lock & Dam 15, the largest roller dam in the world (top). A captain pilots a towboat past the open swing span of the Crescent railroad bridge between Davenport and Rock Island (bottom).

Oregionality

When winter weather breaks, steam rises from the Mississippi River under the Interstate-74 Bridge between Bettendorf and Moline (top). A stunning view from the steep bluffs of the Mississippi Palisades State Park north of Savanna (bottom).

William Mannhardt

In the midst of daily living, one young girl takes time to enjoy the view (top). Sailors take in the great riverfront scenery, including Quarters One at the Rock Island Arsenal, the second largest home owned by the U.S. government (bottom). Only the White House is bigger.

Kathy Thompson

Oregionality

Our countryside is full of surprises, such as this hot-air balloon soaring over a farm pond in rural Scott County (top). A contrast in cultures: John O'Meara of Bettendorf speeds through his Gameboy challenges as a barge lazes down the river near the Lindsey Park boat docks in Davenport (bottom).

Jeff Cook

Jeff Cook

A fisherman gets a paddle-wheeling treat as the Twilight quietly passes by upstream from LeClaire (left). Barge work is a tough and demanding life reserved for our more robust residents (right).

Oregionality

A t the far-reaching end of the region lies Lock & Dam 12 in Bellevue, Iowa, another scenic Mississippi River destination (left and right).

R iver transportation moves along unfazed by morning fog on the Mississippi near LeClaire (top). Even when Mother Nature gives our region a slap, good-natured residents go with the flow. While floodwaters aren't funny, this billboard on the sponsor fence at John O'Donnell stadium puts some humor in nature's punch (bottom).

Oregionality

Greg Boll

Jeff Cook

The historic Centennial Bridge, spanning from Rock Island to Davenport, the first four-lane span to cross the Mississippi River, opened in 1940 (top). This sculpture, "Watching the Ferry," by late renowned Quad-City artist John Bloom delights riders and walkers along the bike path near the Village of East Davenport (bottom).

Big barges, big ropes (top). A close-up captures the power of an authentic paddlewheel boat (bottom). Young sailors enjoy a laid-back afternoon on their boat near the Davenport Sailing Club (facing page).

Oregionality

William Taylor

Ed Wilson

Where the river runs west: The sun bids adieu to the region and the Interstate-280 Bridge in west Davenport (top). A gleaming downtown Davenport is experiencing a river renaissance that keeps its streets bustling with nighttime activity (bottom).

Downtown Davenport and Lock & Dam 15 are beautifully mirrored on one of those rare days when the Mississippi is completely calm (top). The sturdy steel of the I-74 bridge between Bettendorf and Moline provides a contrasting backdrop to the delicate petunias of a lovely backyard garden (bottom).

Oregionality

Nancy L. Purington

Only from the air can one imagine the enormity of the Rock Island Arsenal. This birds-eye view is taken from the west; Illinois is on the right, Iowa on the left (facing page top). The two spans of the Interstate 74 Bridge appear monumental from below in these dramatic photos, captured by *Oregionality* cover photographer Dan Wallace (facing page bottom). The calm waters of this inlet on the Mississippi River south of Lock & Dam 14 in LeClaire make it a favorite ice-fishing spot (top). Bald eagles and other birds of prey are fond of the old, tall cottonwood trees that line the shores of our region's rivers, providing them a great view for fishing (bottom).

Nancy L. Purington

Mississippi River Bend

Celebrate & Remember

Craig Chandler

▶ Jeff Cook ▶ Ken Weidenbach

Larry Fisher

The Mississippi River Bend Region loves to celebrate and remember. From riverfront spectaculars to small-town celebrations, you'll always find something happening here. The world-famous Mississippi Valley Blues Festival on the riverbanks of Davenport keeps crowds jumping each Fourth of July weekend (facing page). The Clinton County fair stocks plenty of ribbons for all the winners in its 4-H livestock competitions (top). Clever students at St. Paul Catholic School, Davenport, show their patriotic spirit by creating a flag on the school fence (bottom left). Hero Street Park in Silvis remembers its fallen soldiers every Veteran's Day and year round at the town's memorial park (bottom right).

F uture Farmers of America and 4-H competitors brave the summer heat to face off at the region's many county fairs. Both organizations build our new generation of leaders.

Oregionality

Craig Chandler

Jeff Cook

I n the Mississippi River Bend Region, we dance to the beat of many different drummers. A couple swings to Dixieland music at the Bix Beiderbecke Memorial Jazz Festival in Davenport's LeClaire Park (top). A little senorita gets a dance lesson as crowds celebrate Hispanic culture at the Viva Quad Cities Fiesta on John Deere Commons in Moline (bottom left). The Rock Island Metro Youth Precision Drill Team keeps these entertaining, high-stepping kids busy at parades and in competitions (bottom right).

Oregionality

Jeff Cook

John Schultz

T he blues are gonna getcha, but in a really great way, at the annual riverfront Mississippi Valley Blues Festival in Davenport (top). This Clinton High School band director uses body language to get her young talent ready for a big parade (bottom).

Bix, Bix and more Bix. The annual Bix Beiderbecke Jazz Festival in Davenport is just one of the featured attractions as the region celebrates the talents of its native son, Bix, a world-renowned coronet player. Palmer College of Chiropractic students walk in the Quad-City Times Bix 7 Race appropriately costumed as a giant spinal column.

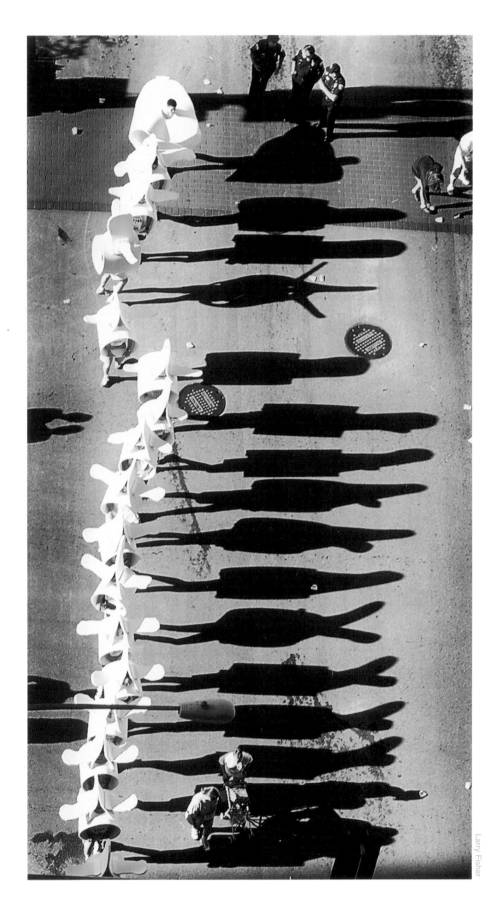

Larry Fisher

Oregionality

orld-class Dixieland jazz reigns during the Bix festival in the historic bandshell of Davenport's riverfront LeClaire Park (top and bottom left). Wells Fargo, sponsor of the Bix weekend street festival, is front and center as a little girl soars in front of the company's historic bank building (top right), and a young lady looks squeamish as she takes part in one of the many fun and unusual fest activities (bottom right).

T hings are always looking up when the region celebrates flying machines. The Steerman Fly In at Gen-Air Park in Geneseo is just like a big family reunion (top). A group from the Make-A-Wish Foundation views some high-flying fun at the enormous Quad-City Air Show at the Davenport Municipal Airport (bottom).

Jeff Cook

Ethel Coffman

For some old-fashioned fun, a reenactment of the Underground Railroad delivers some fascinating history (top). At Pine Grist Mill Heritage Days in Muscatine, Chuck Herman provides free rides on his horse-powered wagon (bottom).

The region is a patriot's dream. We honor the red, white and blue in parades (top left and right), and at the Rock Island Arsenal National Cemetery, where scouts place flags on each veteran's grave on Memorial Day (bottom).

Jeff Cook

Jeff Cook

Greg Boll

Oregionality

Greg Boll

royal Neighbors of America and Modern Woodmen of America, both fraternal benefit societies headquartered in Rock Island, annually remind us of our patriotic responsibilities during a Flag Day celebration (top). Lincoln Fundamental School kids do the wave – the flag wave, that is – at Davenport's annual Veteran's Day Parade (bottom).

Craig Chandler

Mississippi River Bend

The capacity crowd digs Cher at The Mark of the Quad-Cities in Moline (top). The Dutch sweep the town, wooden shoes and all, at the annual Dutch Days in Fulton (bottom left). Crazy competition keeps these young women in stitches (bottom right).

Jeff Cook

Melissa Haegele

Craig Chandler

Oregionality

he annual Celtic Highland
Games of the Quad-Cities
are always an eye-opener.
From bagpipers (top) to the sheaf-toss
competition (bottom right) to people
watching (bottom left), this ethnic tradition grows bigger every year at the
Mississippi Valley Fairgrounds in
Davenport.

John Schultz

Stephanie Willcox

Nate Ullrich

When summer turns to fall, Megan Ewoldt makes her own fun out of plentiful fallen leaves (left). Regional weddings range from traditional (top right) to not-so-ordinary (bottom right).

Oregionality

What can you say about fair fare?
Mmm, mmm, good!

T iny tikes make like Dorothy at the Toto Fest in DeWitt, Iowa (top). Trick or treating is still a safe tradition in the Midwest, including at Carriage Place Estates in Bettendorf (bottom). The Quad City Air Show has become one of the region's most highly attended celebrations, featuring every type of airplane from vintage and stunt crafts to our military's finest fleets, including the Navy's Blue Angels (facing page).

Oregionality

Mississippi River Bend

Greg Boll

Ed Wilson

P opular *Quad-City Times* columnist Bill Wundram proves he's full of blarney at The Grand Parade, which traverses the Centennial Bridge between Rock Island and Davenport on St. Patrick's Day weekend (top left). An Irish mother makes sure she'll be noticed on the parade route (top right). Things get a little more serious at one of the region's Civil War reenactments (bottom right).

Jack Vyverberg

Oregionality

egional residents love high-flying events, from the colossal Quad-City Air Show (top) to a simpler school celebration balloon release (bottom).

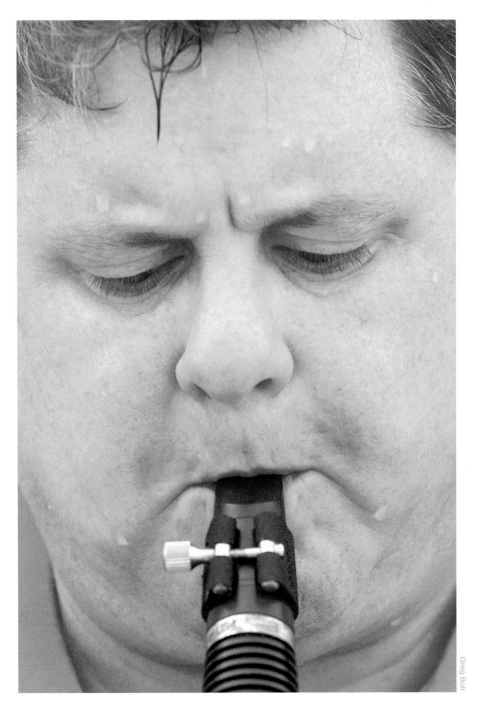

Greg Boll

Jeff Cook

A singer hits the high note at a Davenport river-front festival (right). Whatever the occasion, the region likes to toot its horn (left).

Oregionality

Diane Dexter-Wall

Remembering those who gave their lives for our freedom is never forgotten when visiting the Rock Island Arsenal National Cemetery (top). Our regional festivals are not complete without face painting (bottom).

Tracy Hayes

ecisions, decisions. Santa waits patiently for a young lady to speak her mind at NorthPark Mall in Davenport (top left). Tractors and reindeer – only in Iowa during the Quad-City Arts Festival of Trees Holiday Parade (top right). Fun and entertainment at the annual downtown Muscatine Holiday Stroll (bottom).

Janet Kettelkamp

Greg Boll

Beth Hecht

Oregionality

LeClaire residents come together to raise support for victims of Sept. 11, 2001 (top). Proud veterans keep us hopeful and thankful during the Davenport Veteran's Day Parade (bottom).

Janet Rossmiller-Miller

Jeff Cook

retty maids all ... and ducks ... in a row. The award-winning Back Water Gamblers perform every weekend during hot summers in Rock Island (top). The Great Quad-City Duck Race on the Mississippi River annually raises money for local charities (bottom).

Oregionality

Jeff Cook

When the circus comes to town, the elephant walk is a grand tradition on John Deere Commons in Moline (top). The Quad-City Sports Center in Davenport is a Shangri-la for up-and-coming stars of the ice (bottom left). The Quad City Symphony and our area ice-skating talent join forces for the Holiday Pops Concert at Moline's Mark of the Quad-Cities (bottom right).

Larry Fisher

Jeff Cook

Greg Boll

When bald eagles come to town for the winter, the region celebrates at various events including Bald Eagle Days at Rock Island's QCCA Expo Center (top). A young talent at the annual Quad-Cities Jugglefest at Davenport's RiverCenter practices his own version of high-flying fun (bottom).

Jeff Cook

I n The District of Rock Island, a unique downtown area devoted to arts and entertainment, festivals and events are on the bill all year-round (top and bottom).

The Thirst To Win

Greg Boll

John Schultz ▲
Greg Boll ▼

Jeff Cook

Determination marks the face of a Clinton High School soccer player (facing page). Bikers lean into a curve at the Quad-City Criterium, an annual Memorial Day event in the District of Rock Island (top). The annual Mississippi River Tug Fest brings entertainment and events including fireworks, a carnival and a tug-of-war between teams from LeClaire, Iowa, and Port Byron, Ill. A participant gives his all (bottom left). The Komen Race for the Cure® is an annual fund-raiser benefiting research for the cure of breast cancer. Fun, exercise and supporting a good cause enthuse a group of walkers (bottom right).

Matthew Wince won third place in the *Oregionality* photo contest for this action-filled image of a young flag football player dodging opponents during YMCA competition in Davenport (top). Steamwheelers arena football is a fan favorite on the Quad-Cities' sports scene. Taking football indoors, the team is part of the Arena Football League 2 (af2), the training league for the AFL. Here, a Steamwheeler leaps for a catch (bottom).

Oregionality

H igh school sports stir team spirit and rivalry in students, parents, teachers and alumni on both sides of the river. Cheerleaders get fans and players pumped up in preparation for a Clinton High School game (top). An Assumption Knight lunges for extra yardage before being taken down by North Scott's defense (bottom).

Greg Ball

John Schultz

▲ John Schultz
▼ Jeff Cook

E ach year, the Quad-City Times Bix 7 road race provides running excitement for thousands. Athletes face the July heat, hordes of fellow competitors and a seven-mile course filled with hills (facing page). Water mist provides welcome relief to a Junior Bix runner (top left) and athletes tackling a Bix at Six training run (top right). The Alcoa Junior Bix gives aspiring racers a taste of the action (bottom).

D avenport's River Bandits, an affiliate of the Minnesota Twins, give baseball enthusiasts a chance to catch pros in action. Baseballs autographed by the team await distribution to spectators (top). A River Bandit catcher tries to block an elusive ball (bottom).

Jeff Cook

A majestic skyline provides a backdrop for the last hit of a neighborhood game in Bettendorf.

Jeff Cook

Greg Ball

F ans will do almost anything to spur their team to victory, from baring bellies to painting faces (top, bottom and facing page).

Oregionality

A figure skater impresses an audience of one at the Quad-City Sports Center (top left). Not this time! A goalie thwarts an attempt to score (top right). Charlie has the equipment he needs, but seems bewildered by the monumental task of getting that little puck into the goal (bottom).

Oregionality

S miles on ice: Skaters race to the finish at the Vander Veer Park Silver Skates Competition (top). A helmet becomes an impromptu shower at United Township High School football practice (bottom left). A sack-race winner stretches for the finish line (bottom right).

Air-bound snow lovers find the best jumps at SnowStar Winter Sports Park in Andalusia.

Greg Boll

Greg Boll

Greg Boll

O r e g i o n a l i t y

Quad-City Mallards hockey draws thousands of fans each season. A Mallard glove is discarded as confrontation interrupts play (top). Down but not out: A Mallard is on the ice, but definitely still in the game (middle). Our beloved winning Mallards clinched the league championship in 2001, 1998 and 1997 (bottom).

Davenport's John O'Donnell Stadium offers a great view of River Bandits baseball and the Centennial Bridge spanning the Mississippi River between Davenport and Rock Island.

Oregionality

A men's fast-pitch softball player winds up for the release (top left). An up-and-coming athlete finds a soft seat while receiving instruction (top middle). Friends help celebrate a victory for the Muscatine High School softball team (top right). Unfazed by a curtain of dangling legs, a River Bandit waits to bat (bottom).

Basketball is a favorite pastime for players, fans and friends. All dressed up and ready to win: A Bellevue-Marquette student decks out for his favorite team at the Iowa State Tournament (top left). Kids find time for some hoops at the Bridgeview Elementary School playground in LeClaire (top right). Bettendorf High School cheerleaders whip up team spirit for the Bulldogs (bottom).

Oregionality

John Schultz

B asketball, both organized and "on the street," plays a big role in our communities.

A bug's-eye view captures the whole field at a men's fast-pitch softball game (top). A batter slides into first, stirring a cloud of dust (bottom).

240

A high school high jumper exceeds the bar (top). One last push to the finish line at the Quad-City Times Bix 7 (bottom left) and at a track meet at the Brady Street Stadium (bottom right).

he Quad City Rowing Association takes advantage of cool summer mornings to knife through the waters of the Mississippi River.

Oregionality

The Backwater Gamblers water skiers compete nationally, in addition to providing exciting entertainment on the Rock River in Rock Island. Here, skiers show their incredible talent (top). Athletes splash into position at the Quad-Cities Triathlon at West Lake Park in Davenport (bottom).

Players end a soccer game with a splash in Clinton (top left). Grimacing, a Pleasant Valley Spartan intercepts a pass (top right). OOPS! An aspiring goalie sheepishly confronts a wayward ball (bottom left). Braving a contact sport without pads, Palmer College of Chiropractic rugby players get rough and rowdy (bottom right).

John Schultz

Greg Boll

Jeff Cook

Greg Boll

Oregionality

A rollerblader soars into the night sky at Bettendorf's skateboard park (top). And they're off! The Rock Island Grand Prix draws drivers from all over the world to participate in 14 exciting racing events through The District of Rock Island (bottom).

John Schultz

As you can see, golf is really big in the region! In fact, Golf Digest rated the Quad-Cities No. 1 nationally for affordability and easy access among cities with populations between 250,000 and a million (left). Each year, golfers from all over the world congregate for the John Deere Classic. The event is a stop on the PGA tour, attracting professional players, many of whom are ranked in the top 50 golfers in the nation. In 2002, the John Deere Classic raised $1.45 million for more than 500 local charities (top and bottom right).

Tracy Hayes

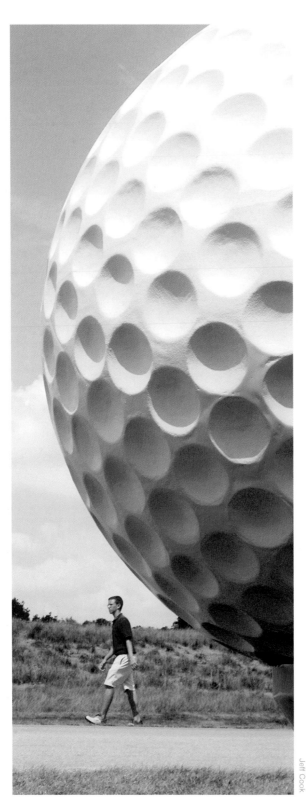

Jeff Cook

Greg Boll

Oregionality

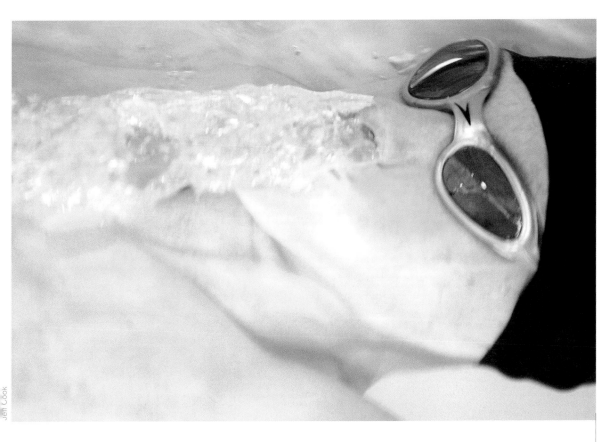

A swimmer concentrates on maintaining a perfect streamline (top). Teamwork is the only way to victory for crews competing at the Quad-City Rowing Regatta, one of several sculling events held in the fall each year (bottom).

spectator has an impressive view as thousands wait for the start of the Quad-City Times Bix 7 race.

Oregionality

A grand entrance goes awry for a moment at Alleman High School (top). Control and agility send Assumption High School cheerleaders on their way to winning the state cheering competition for the seventh year in a row (middle). Preston, Iowa, girls get a meaningful reminder as they exit the locker room for a big game (bottom).

Greg Boll

Sharon Barrett

Craig Chandler

Jeff Cook

John Schultz ▲
▼ Jeff Cook

They said they would come, and they did. The building of the IMAX Theatre marked the beginning of a new era of high-tech culture in the region (facing page). Late Quad-City Sculptor Isabel Bloom's legacy continues in a brilliantly renovated historic building storefront on John Deere Commons in Moline (top). Built next to the Mississippi River in downtown Rock Island, the Quad City Botanical Center is a gardener's dream come true for the region (bottom).

Mike Denning

Don Richhart III

The Heritage Place office building in Moline marked the beginning of that city's downtown revitalization (top). Ushering in a new era of health care, Trinity Regional Health System introduced an aesthetically pleasing residential-style hospital setting at its 7th Street Campus in Moline (bottom).

Oregionality

The 12,000-seat Mark of the Quad Cities introduced regional residents to big-arena events from professional sports to top celebrity performers (top). This impressive skywalk and its beautiful surroundings connect the world-class Genesis Heart Center, forefront, to the main Genesis Medical Center East hospital (bottom).

istorically accurate restoration of four faces of the clock in the U.S. Army Corps of Engineers headquarters Clock Tower Building on Rock Island's Arsenal Island was an adventure in time for contractors, including Dave Virgil of Del Jen, who gives the minute hand a spin while testing its accuracy. The clock has kept time for Quad-Citians since 1868 (top and bottom). The Isle of Capri Hotel raised the bar for sophistication by creating a resort-style setting to complement its riverboat casino along the Mississippi Riverfront in Bettendorf (facing page top). Named one of the 54 Best Inns in America by National Geographic Traveler magazine, The Abbey Hotel, constructed in Bettendorf between 1914-17 as a monastery, provides luxury accommodations atop one of the highest bluffs overlooking the Mississippi River valley (facing page bottom).

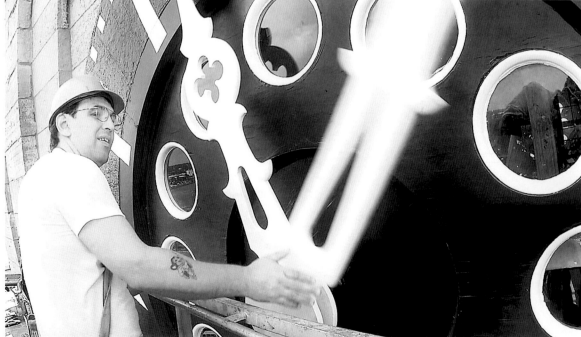

Ed Wilson

William Taylor

Mississippi River Bend

Quinn Kirkpatrick

The region's favorite festival playground is the historic band shell on the riverfront of Davenport's LeClaire Park.

Oregionality

 he warming house at the Prospect Park lagoon in Moline has thawed the toes of many an ice skater through the years.

Many companies in the region exist to serve larger manufacturers. Here a worker paints augers (bottom), and they're ready for shipment to a John Deere factory (top).

Oregionality

A look to the top of the region's round barns can make you dizzy (top). Another building going up, a common site in today's Mississippi River Bend Region (bottom).

Jeff Cook

Jeff Cook

Our cultural venues just keep getting better. In Davenport, despite the Putnam Museum's new ultra-modern exterior (top left), inside visitors discover the treasures of regional and world history (bottom right). In Rock Island, the Quad City Botanical Center transports visitors to the tropics inside its amazing 6,444 square foot Sun Garden conservatory (top right). The Family Museum of Arts and Science in Bettendorf makes learning fun. Requirement for admission: Imagination! (facing page).

Oregionality

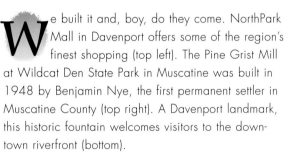

W e built it and, boy, do they come. NorthPark Mall in Davenport offers some of the region's finest shopping (top left). The Pine Grist Mill at Wildcat Den State Park in Muscatine was built in 1948 by Benjamin Nye, the first permanent settler in Muscatine County (top right). A Davenport landmark, this historic fountain welcomes visitors to the downtown riverfront (bottom).

Oregionality

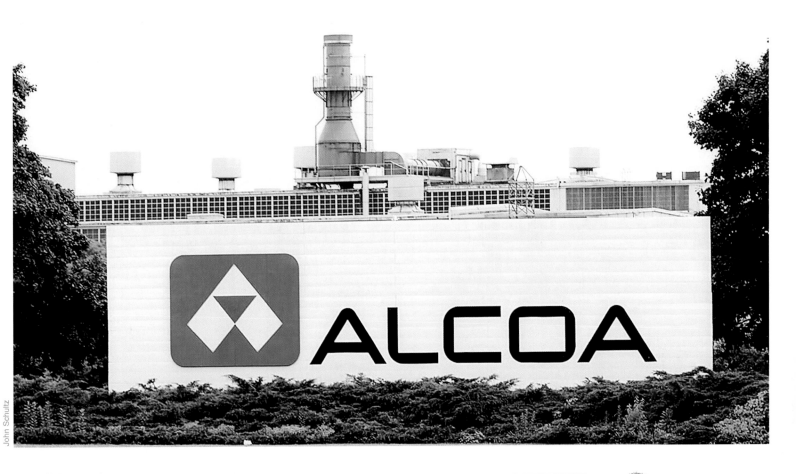

John Schultz

Jeff Cook

Mammoth Alcoa Davenport Works, one of the region's largest employers, sprawls for more than a mile along the riverfront in Riverdale (top). With great attention to detail, this craftsman is creating with his hands the vision that is in his mind (bottom).

Greg Boll ▲
▼ Greg Boll

Craig Chandler

Nancy L. Purington

Mama never told him there'd be days like this – a worker makes the long climb up the under-construction 1,000 foot WQAD broadcast tower in Orion (facing page). Two youngsters appear to be looking out for lions and tigers and bears as they stroll the brick road of the Quad City Botanical Center in Rock Island (top left). Incredible house-of-worship architecture across the region can take your breath away (top right). The Great River Bank in Princeton caters to boaters with unique float-up banking (bottom).

ulton's Dutch windmill, "De Immigrant," is the only authentic Dutch working windmill in Illinois and, currently, only the second in the United States (facing page). The support columns of the Interstate-80 Bridge in LeClaire take on the appearance of a mysterious multi-roomed tomb (top). This riverfront sculpture in the Village of East Davenport is an artist's interpretation of the multitude of architectural styles in the Quad-City area (bottom).

Larry Fisher

Jeff Cook

Greg Boll

Oregionality

M ississippi Boulevard, one of the last remaining historic brick streets in Davenport, still carries modern-day carriages up bluffy hills (facing top left). A dearly loved home avoids the development wrecking ball by escaping to a new location (facing top right). Grand historic homes and neighborhoods continue to be meticulously restored to their full splendor by a new generation of home buyers (facing bottom). Fulton's Heritage Canyon covered bridge is part of a 12-acre wooded nature walk that transports visitors into a recreated 1860s log cabin settlement (above).

D avenport's busy Brady Street Stadium plays host to myriad school events from football games to band competitions.

Oregionality

R emembering a hero: This statue of Sauk warrior Black Hawk was erected in 1892 in what is now Black Hawk State Park in Rock Island. The park contains more than 200 hilly, wooded acres that back up to the Rock River.

Oregionality

E agle Point Park in Clinton, Iowa, sits on a cliff overlooking the Mississippi River. Visitors can climb the stairs of this castle for one of the best river views in the Mississippi River Bend region (top). Built in the late 1800s of red sandstone and granite, the Romanesque-style Clinton County Courthouse features a central tower made of weathered copper (bottom).

Oregionality

Building minds: The Quad-Cities area is blessed to have several colleges and universities nearby. For almost 150 years, Augustana College in Rock Island has been educating students (facing page). St. Ambrose University started as a seminary for young men. Today, it educates both young men and women on its Davenport campus.

D rivers and their teams test their "need for speed" at Cordova Dragway Park in Cordova (top). The annual Venetian Boat Parade illuminates the night sky as creative displays glide along the Mississippi (bottom). Baseball fans taking a break from watching the action at John O'Donnell Stadium in Davenport (facing page).

Oregionality

Mississippi River Bend

All In A Day's Work

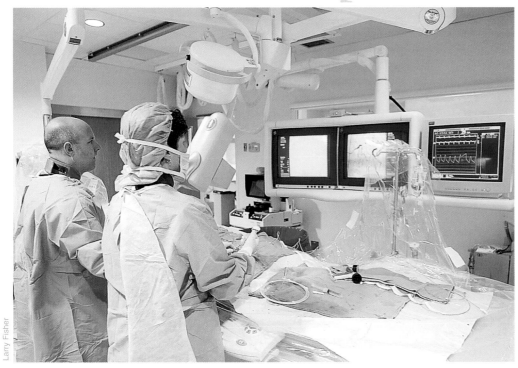

T he job of a Davenport firefighter ranges from risking his life in buildings to saving the life of a cat (facing page). Dr. Eric Dippel and Nurse Kathy Johnson perform heart surgery in the cath lab at Genesis East (top). Three-year-old Alex Venema sits on a squirrel to get his hair cut by Nicole Faso, while 3-year-old Laurence Turner gets a hair cut from Peggy Price in a kid-friendly salon (bottom).

Jeff Cook

Our agricultural heritage is something we share with the world, whether it be juicy, red tomatoes sold from the back of a truck (top) or during a farmer's market (bottom). The Quad-Cities' rich ag legacy includes farm machinery transported throughout the world (facing page top), and corn near Walcott, in rural Scott County (facing page bottom).

HOME GROWN TOMATOES
$7

Jeff Cook

Oregionality

Craig Chandler

John Schultz

Mississippi River Bend   281

Davenport's Palmer College of Chiropractic has sent thousands of its graduates to practice throughout the world. Student extern Wesley Martin adjusts patient Jamila Maddox, while faculty member Dr. Gloria Niles assists. A Moline High School football coach sends his young men into the game with encouraging words (facing page top), while a rail yard employee makes sure a train is ready to roll (facing page bottom).

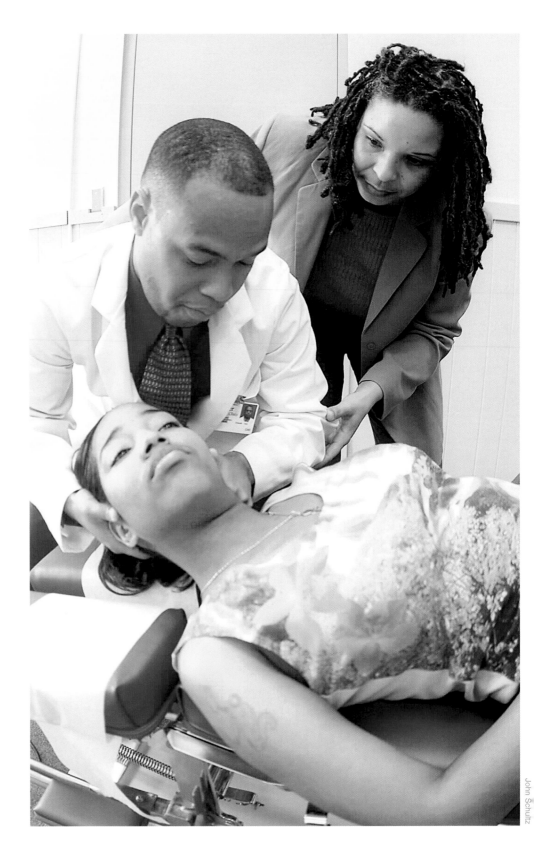

Oregionality

onstruction is one of the signs of a booming economy. Wally Ewoldt of Tracy Construction, Davenport, places roof sheeting on a condo in the Schaeffer Farms addition in Davenport (top). A construction worker takes a break (bottom).

John Schultz

John Schultz

Oregionality

orkers are seen behind plastic sheeting during construction of the new Trinity at Terrace Park hospital in Bettendorf (top). Construction workers place a new steeple on a Lutheran church in Orion (bottom).

Larry Fisher

Greg Boll

Welcome back! Bridgeview Elementary School Principal Michelle Barnes greets a student on the first day of school. A child crosses Valley Drive after getting off the school bus (bottom). An employee of Java Station makes sure commuters get their jolt of caffeine (facing page).

S parks flying is all part of the job for a welder at a Quad-City company (top). A worker takes safety precautions in her job (bottom).

Oregionality

Factory workers are at the heart of manufacturing in the region.

Regional schools prepare our future workforce (top). Mallory Celeste McMichaelis contemplates a medical career as she listens to mother Jenni's heart during a fun night at Bridgeview Elementary School in LeClaire (bottom).

uad-City Times photographer Greg Boll gives the thumbs-up before taking off with a member of the Aeroshell T-6 flight demonstration team (top). The Scott County Sheriff's Posse enjoys its job keeping the masses in line at the annual St. Patrick's Day Parade in Davenport (bottom).

River Gulf Grain employee Ed Maynard operates a chute to carry soybeans from a terminal to a barge and down the Mississippi River.

Oregionality

A Davenport fire captain tackles a house fire.

John Schultz

Quad-City workers are on the job, whether it's cutting hair, building a new store (facing page top) or constructing the carnival (facing page bottom).

Oregionality

T he Midwest work ethic prevails in the region, from line work at the John Deere Harvester plant in East Moline (top) to landscaping (bottom).

Oregionality

A downtown Davenport visitor obeys the parking laws even during a snowstorm (left). A carpenter often faces unexpected surprises on the job (bottom).

Quad-Citians like to go out to eat, as evidenced by the packed parking lots of restaurants all over the area. But have you ever thought how many workers it takes to keep all those eateries humming? Customers see and interact with many of those hard-working servers and bartenders (top and bottom), but countless more labor behind-the-scenes in the kitchens (facing page).

John Schultz

The Rock Island Arsenel is one of the largest employers in the Quad-City area. Most are civilians who work on government contracts (bottom) but a sizeable amount of staff are career military. And in typical military fashion, the leaders are transferred often, resulting in change-of-command ceremonies every couple of years on the island (top).

William Taylor

Oregionality

Workers looking for new jobs get a little help at job fairs. Employers from all over the region gather several times a year to make the match a little easier.

Government works for you. A Medic dispatcher makes sure emergency services are sent to the right place when help is needed urgently (top). A city planner explains how a federal program will benefit the Quad-City region (bottom).

Oregionality

W hen the weekend rolls around, some Quad-Citians head to work. Musicians work when the rest of us want to play – giving us beautiful and fun music at many of the region's festivals and events (top left). Some craftspeople haul their wares from festival to festival. This woman makes pretty necklaces using skills she learned from generations past (top right). Thousands of Quad-City families over the years have made their livings from Deere & Company. These people put their fun in the hands of Deere, and a dutiful driver, too (bottom).

Thousands of Quad-Citians, from teenagers on up, earn money at our retail stores by making the rest of us look better. Businessmen and women know shoes make the person, and this gentleman makes sure they look their best (left). This longtime suit salesman knows how to make his customers look like a million bucks (right).

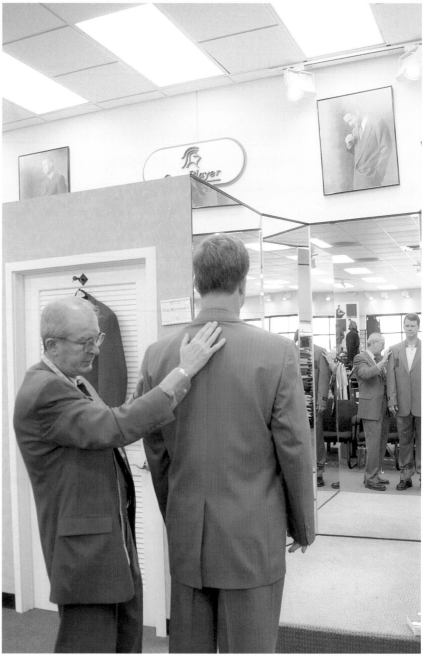

Oregionality

John Schultz

When someone needs a hand, Quad-Citians respond. This young mother and daughter needed a place to live, and Habitat for Humanity – and its dozens of volunteers – came to fulfill their dream of homeownership.

Community & Corporate Profiles

THE BEST OF EASTERN IOWA & WESTERN ILLINOIS

A LOOK AT SOME OF THE COMMUNITIES AND ELITE ORGANIZATIONS
THAT HAVE HELPED BUILD THE REGION AND MAKE THIS BOOK POSSIBLE.

ALCOA DAVENPORT WORKS

At right, the 1.25 mile-long Davenport Works facility has 126 acres under roof – about the size of an 18-hole golf course. Below, this huge aluminum coil measures 96 inches in diameter and out-weighs conventional 54-inch diameter counterparts, shown behind, by 20,000 pounds. Also below, Alcoa's 100-inch hot rolling mill proved itself as the heart of Davenport Works quality improvement efforts in the 1990s.

furnaces bubble with molten aluminum, overhead cranes move massive trays of metal, and huge rolling mills take two-feet-thick ingots and reduce them to less than an inch – is part of Alcoa Inc., the world's leading producer of primary aluminum, fabricated aluminum and alumina. More than 127,000 Alcoans work in 40 countries.

At Davenport Works, 2,100 Alcoans produce aluminum products for the world's aerospace, automotive, trucking, lighting, defense, computer and printing industries.

Since 1948, Alcoa Davenport Works' state-of-the-art equipment and skilled workforce have propelled the company into the forefront of the metals industry. The scope of its technology and differentiated product mix are unparalleled in the world.

How Aluminum Is Made

Davenport Works makes an amazing 10,000 specifications using more than 100 different alloys. Inside Alcoa's giant ingot plant, the process begins. Metals are melted and mixed and impurities removed. The molten metal is cooled in molds, forming ingots cast in lengths up to an astonishing 30 feet. Each one meets an individual customer's exact specifications. In its four hot rolling mills, including the world's most advanced 100-inch continuous mill, the metal is hot rolled at about 900 degree in a series of passes to decrease thickness and dramatically increase length.

After exiting the hot line some coils are rolled to final thickness, but most are sent for further processing in the plate mill or cold rolling mills. Rolling metal at room temperature is called cold rolling. This process further reduces the metal's thickness, producing quality characteristics not always achievable by hot rolling.

The plate mill then heat treats, stretches, artificially ages, machines and cuts aluminum plate to final dimensions. Its prowess includes giant, computerized milling machines, which precisely trim and taper airplane wings more than 100 feet long.

Innovation and Ideas

Throughout its history, Alcoa Davenport Works has set new standards for engineering excellence. Even the plant's construction is a testimony to the versatility of aluminum. Alcoa used 3,125 tons of aluminum to construct the plant's walls and roof. It was the single largest application of aluminum in the history of building trades.

Alcoa achieves manufacturing excellence through constant change that is essential to meeting current and future customer demands.

During the 1990s, Davenport Works reinvested more than $500 million in technological improvements. Part of the investment was the plant's 1996 installation of the largest vertical heat-treating furnace in North America. The furnace processes aluminum sheet up to 44 inches wide and 500 inches long, tripling the plant's capacity for wide aerospace fuselage sheet.

Prestige Projects

When the United States went to war in the Persian Gulf in 1991, so did Alcoa Davenport Works aluminum. Sheet and plate products were used in aircraft carriers, amphibious landing vehicles, airplanes, helicopters and dozens of other vehicles and supplies. That impressive list is just the tip of Alcoa's high-profile projects iceberg.

Davenport Works was the only place in the world that could produce a single piece of aluminum wide enough to form a 209-inch circle to use in the fabrication of the fuel tank domes for the Delta IV rocket – the biggest Delta-series rocket ever built. The plant supplied the largest heat-treated aluminum plate ever rolled for Boeing 747 Jumbo Jets. Each plate weighed more than 10,000 pounds. NASA employed thousands of pounds of Davenport Works aluminum for the external fuel tanks of its space shuttles. Locally, the Scott County Courthouse in Davenport was the world's first aluminum-clad courthouse and set trends in architecture.

Environmental Stewardship

As neighbors of the Mississippi River, Davenport Alcoans, both as a workforce and as individuals, understand and appreciate their obligation to preserve the air, water and wildlife resources for future generations.

The company's involvement in the environment takes many forms. They include large-budget and technically intensive solutions, such as working to achieve ISO 14001 certification that encompasses strict environmental protection standards.

The company is deeply committed to preventing pollution as well as illness and injury. Equally important is its support for the smaller scale environmental projects and efforts of the community and Alcoa employees. These include land conservation, tree and seed planting and cleanup programs.

The Alcoa Family

Alcoans always have been ready to step up to the next challenge, a new direction in business or the next innovation in technology.

Empowered by management to make decisions themselves, Alcoans take pride in ownership in and responsibility for excellence in all they do.

The company encourages its employees to make a positive impact on their community and build strong families. Davenport Works provides myriad opportunities for them to do so in education, recreation and family-oriented volunteerism and activities.

With all Alcoans at Davenport working together and doing their best, the future looks bright for this fascinating facility that calls the Quad-Cities home.

Above, Alcoa is a major supporter of Chad Pregracke's Living Lands and Water, which organizes community volunteers to clean up waste from our nation's rivers. Below, Alcoa sheet and plate products help create Hum-Vees for the Army.

Alcoa Davenport Works

**4879 State Street
Riverdale, Iowa 52722
(563) 459-2001
www.alcoa.com**

LINKING LEARNING TO LIFE. THIS IS MORE THAN A THEME IN THE BETTENDORF COMMUNITY SCHOOL DISTRICT. IT REFLECTS THE RIGOR AND RELEVANCE OF A UNIQUE AND DYNAMIC EDUCATIONAL ORGANIZATION.

BETTENDORF COMMUNITY SCHOOL DISTRICT

Ray Stensvad
  Administration Center
3311 Central Avenue
Bettendorf, Iowa 52722
(563) 359-3681
www.bettendorf.k12.ia.us

Excellence has been a tradition in this school district since its inception. Its mission, in partnership with students' families and the community, is to develop well-rounded students who have the ability to reason and act in an ethical manner so they can make a living, make a life and make a difference.

To achieve its high goals, this flagship school district continually implements progressive initiatives that emphasize the education of the whole child. Its success is evident. Districtwide, the Bettendorf schools have a daily attendance rate of about 96 percent with a graduation rate of more than 95 percent. Bettendorf students consistently score in the high-performance level nationally on both the Iowa Tests of Basic Skills and

Above, Bettendorf grade schoolers participate in many enrichment programs, including tree planting. Above, top, Bettendorf Middle School helps kids build confidence and skill through innovative activities such as rock-wall climbing. Right, at Bettendorf High School, educators place emphasis on active, applied learning and the integration of school-to-work/career opportunities curriculum.

the Iowa Tests of Educational Development. About 85 percent of Bettendorf graduates attend post-secondary institutions.

Success in All Shapes and Sizes

The Bettendorf Community School District is comprised of six elementary schools, including one building on a balanced/extended-year calendar, one middle school, one high school and an alternative high school program.

Successful strategic initiatives apply at all levels of education. A small sampling includes:

Preschool: The Birth-to-Five Program provides parents with a vast array of resources and information, such as parent education, preschool story times, infant/toddler tummy time and family fun nights.

Elementary: Breakthrough to Literacy, a unique learning enrichment opportunity, provides thousands of customized lessons with instant feedback through interactive software.

Middle School: The House System is an interdisciplinary structure used to provide each student with more personal educational delivery. Teachers share common planning time, enabling them to consult with one another for many purposes, including interdisciplinary instruction, special event planning and field trips. The program structure allows teachers to spend extra time meeting the needs of individual students. Additionally, the middle school offers one house with a looping component. Students in this house have an opportunity to remain with their teachers for multiple years.

High School: Block Scheduling provides larger blocks of instruction time spent on subjects that provide a more flexible and productive classroom environment. Teachers incorporate many opportunities for using varied and interactive instruction methods. Benefits include more effective use of school time, decreased class size and an increased number of course offerings. Teachers have more daily interaction with fewer students, allowing them to implement more process-oriented strategies.

Continuous Improvement

The initiatives above and dozens of other intelligent strategic directions attract, develop and retain competent, dedicated and caring professionals who continue to respond to the diverse needs of Bettendorf learners and the high expectations of the community.

By proactively responding to changing fiscal conditions, spending wisely and developing strong community partnerships, the Bettendorf Community School District continues its quest as a flagship district of high-quality educational programs that meet the changing needs of students while maintaining high academic standards.

Oregionality

E NHANCING THE WELLNESS OF THE COMMUNITY STANDS AT THE FOREFRONT OF EVERY DECISION MADE BY THE CITY GOVERNMENT OF BETTENDORF, IOWA. TO RESIDENTS AND NEWCOMERS, IT IS BECOMING THE CITY OF CHOICE FOR QUALITY LIVING.

**1609 State Street
Bettendorf, Iowa 52722
(563) 344-4000
www.bettendorf.org**

Government philosophy, under the direction of Mayor Ann Hutchinson for more than 15 years, spearheads the evolution of Bettendorf as a clean, model city with involved, friendly residents, an efficient responsible city government, excellent cultural and fitness environments and an affordable broad-based tax structure.

Originally named Lillienthal in 1840, then Gilbert in 1858, it was at the turn of the 20th century when brothers William and Joseph Bettendorf proposed moving their growing iron wagon business from neighboring Davenport – but only if the town folk provided land to relocate their factory. Residents and businesses raised funds, the factory prospered and the name of the city was changed in honor of the brothers who were so important to the early development of the community.

The Premier City to Live

N ow, more than 32,000 residents of this community that has the lowest crime rate in the Quad-City metropolitan area share the successes of Bettendorf. No longer considered an unofficial suburb of Davenport, Bettendorf is a viable, growing city.

Its former "suburb" status is reflected in the predominantly residential makeup of the communi

ty. With almost 140 new housing starts in 2003, residential growth continues to lead Bettendorf's expansion. However, considerable economic development efforts are paying off as business and industry recognize the values of serving this young demographic where the average age is about 35 and 18 percent of the population is age 14 and younger.

With anchor store Home Depot leading the revitalization efforts at the former Duck Creek Plaza, the prospects are great for this commercial corridor along Middle and Kimberly roads. Phase two of the project is designed to attract not just full mall capacity, but also a conglomerate of small out-lot stores. More attempts to build its commercial and industrial base include plans for downtown and the expanding 53rd Avenue, as well as I-80 and Middle Road corridors.

And soon, Bettendorf residents will no longer be able to joke that no one is really from the city. With the 2004 opening of its own state-of-the-art, full-service hospital, Trinity at Terrace Park, newborns there will be the first in modern-day history to claim Bettendorf as their place of birth.

Dedicated to Learning and Leisure

A s Bettendorf continues to progress, other elements that

define the city are firmly rooted. For example, the heart and soul of the community lie in its dedication to learning. Its school systems rank as some of the best in the country, and its Learning Campus, an exciting geographical merger of the Bettendorf Public Library and the Family Museum of Arts and Science, has proven itself as a regional showplace for lifelong learning.

Its 20 city parks are beautiful and functional and also include special facilities such as the Life Fitness Center, Palmer Hills Golf Course, a newly opened Family Aquatic Center, two boat-launch areas along the Mississippi River, a 35,000-square-foot Community Center and a 10,000-square-foot skate park. The city has invested more than $13 million in its leisure facilities and parks system over the past 10 years. To residents of Bettendorf, its all about quality of life, and with more and more comforts coming their way, the city is well on the way to achieving its vision as "The Premier City to Live."

Above, Bettendorf's Splash Landing Family Aquatic Center is the place to be for good times in the heat of summer. Above left, Bettendorf is known for its family friendly neighborhoods where good schools, lots of recreation options and safety are highly attractive attributes. Below, the pride and joy of this learning-for-life-oriented community, the Bettendorf Learning Campus, encompasses the Bettendorf Library and the Family Museum of Arts and Science.

I T BECOMES QUITE CLEAR A COMPANY IS PROGRESSIVE WHEN ITS PRESIDENT CAN STATE WITH TOTAL CONFIDENCE THAT HIS ORGANIZATION IS ON THE FAST TRACK OF LEADING-EDGE TECHNOLOGY. THE BRANDT COMPANY LIKES TO BE IN THAT EXTREME POSITION. AS ONE OF THE LARGEST

commercial sheet-fed printers in the Quad-Cities, Brandt is attracting the loyalty of a multitude of regional clients seeking high-profile – even elaborate – printing through customized creative solutions.

President Marc Brandt says adding true value is what his company is determined to deliver. Brandt's vast in-house capabilities and highly team-oriented staff help push the envelope when it comes to setting Brandt apart from the competition.

Investing in Growth

I t is Brandt's continual investment in the right people, training and technologies that are creating myriad advantages for customers. The combination is turning out sharper, cleaner, more vibrant images than were ever thought possible in the world of traditional printing. Moreover, Brandt's high-tech and unique in-house capabilities are actually driving down client costs – a true win-win situation.

Brandt credits the success of the company's continual-reinvestment philosophy to his father Don, who started the business in 1970 with his cousin Bob Brandt. In the

beginning, Brandt supplied, of all things, engineering products to municipalities, industry, architects and the like.

In its early days, a surge of client inquiries for printed business cards prompted Brandt's can-do founders to purchase a small duplicating press. When the company's largest client downsized just

about the same time computers began to replace engineering staples such as drafting tables and T-squares, the two partners began rethinking the value of Brandt's original services.

In 1980, they redirected their focus to printing, and the rest is history. Today, Marc and his brother Bill run the company. Whereas Marc always took a keen interest in the business and computer side of the family operation, Bill became more astute with the production process.

The two talents merged easily into their predecessors' shoes, Marc as president and Bill as vice president of manufacturing. Together, they continue the tradition of continual growth via leading-edge technology.

What began in a 12-by-12-square foot room has matured into a 30,000-square foot manufacturing and distribution facility.

To gain a better understanding how the Brandt business strategy has served the company, consider the following:

In 1980, The Brandt Company could print 264,000 8-by-11-inch, one-color/one-sided sheets per

THE BRANDT COMPANY

Above, The Brandt Company team at the Davenport headquarters. At center, printing technology may change, but not the company name: Current owners, brothers Marc, left, and Bill Brandt mirror the photo of original company owners, their dad Don, left, and his cousin Bob Brandt. The latter two are now retired. Below, Prepress Supervisor Al Larson, right, and Shelly Carnine utilize an all-digital PDF workflow. Plate information is sent electronically to the pressroom using the latest CIP3 technology.

day. In 2003, it can produce 1.856-million 8-by-11-inch, four-color/one-sided sheets per day.

To achieve the increased production, advanced computerized technology has eliminated some of the timely and costly steps of the printing process. For instance, instead of creating film to make a printing plate, Brandt's complete digital workflow takes art directly from computer to plate.

Bringing It In-House

Hand-in-hand with Brandt's high-tech processes is its will to maintain control of the entire printed project, from conception through mailing.

Many solitary capabilities in the printing business such as embossing, foil stamping and mailing services, are typically subcontracted to specialty companies. Brandt takes a different approach. If it makes economic sense, equipment is purchased to produce such specialty applications in-house. The decision to do so is eliminating delays, mistakes and miscommunications.

Passion for Excellence

Choosing to be the exception in the marketplace means Brandt must incorporate a tremendous amount of expertise and skills into its workforce. Marc calls his staff "second to none" whose number one goal is to exceed the expectations of customers at all levels.

Brandt employees have a passion to do just that. The team works together fluidly to achieve the finest outcome on each project. Analytical, technical and experienced are all superlatives Marc uses to define his employees. His veteran sales force, for example, keeps clients educated on new approaches to printing techniques that help marketing materials stand above the crowd. And although press operations are highly automated, his skilled press operators' knowledge of the lithographic process allows them to fine-tune the presses to retain exceptional quality throughout a press run.

Brandt's flexibility throughout the entire process allows the company to meet what used to be unthinkable deadlines. Once a 12-day window was required to complete a typical print project. When urgency requires, that window can be reduced to just a few working days. Even so, the company is operating 24 hours a day, five days a week to meet customer demands.

Clear Vision

The future is already more than a vision for The Brandt Company. The plant is physically expanding to allow for growth in both administration and manufacturing.

To survive the speed of change without sacrificing quality, Brandt incorporates integral quality initiatives that have earned it ISO 9001-2000 status. This internationally recognized certification program sets standards by which customers assess a company's ability to meet certain quality-related criteria. Brandt is one of only about 400 of 44,000 printing companies in the U.S. that has earned this status.

Brandt predicts the next "leading edge" to be pursued is personalization of the printing process that allows direct mail to look the same, but contain customized content based on market demographics.

The company's commitment to quality and change also extends deeply into the communities that embrace Brandt as a leading provider of printing and fulfillment services. To show its gratitude, Brandt contributes to and participates in many community causes, numerous foundations and cultural endeavors.

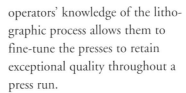

Above, Rocky Jones operates a guillotine cutter. CIP4 technology will be added in the near future to create a complete computer-integrated manufacturing environment. Top left, Second Shift Pressman Brian Mumm runs one of Brandt's four multi-color sheet-fed presses. Closed-loop densitometry systems keep color consistent and accurate. Bottom left, Second Shift Bindery Supervisor Mike Arnold, left, and Jerry Agnew operate one of three high-precision folders. Operators abide by ISO standards and procedures to ensure quality control never is jeopardized.

THE BRANDT COMPANY

3020 Hickory Grove Road
Davenport, Iowa 52806
(563) 386-9740
(800) 720-9740
www.brandtco.com

CARLETON LIFE SUPPORT SYSTEMS, INC.

Above right, Life Support Technician Jeff Brown calibrates a prototype breathing regulator in the regulator laboratory. Below right, Technician Denny Roth assembles a Ceramic Oxygen Generation System integrated manifold and tube assembly in the Ceramic Oxygen Generation Systems laboratory. Below left, this sample of Life Support life-saving products, clockwise from center, includes a Patient Ventilation Oxygen Concentrating System, two On Board Inert Gas Generating Systems, Integrated Manifold and Tube Assembly, two Linear Cryogenic Coolers and the F-16 On Board Oxygen Generation System, which is comprised of an oxygen concentrator, a breathing regulator, a plenum and a back-up oxygen bottle.

When top guns take flight, Life Support oxygen-on-demand technology protects them at high altitudes and during extreme high-g combat maneuvers. When heat-seeking missiles endanger pilots in flight, advanced infrared systems that incorporate Life Support's cryogenic coolers enable the IR system to track, identify and defeat incoming missiles, sending them off course.

When slow, low-flying aircraft, such as rescue helicopters, hover over a war-torn battlefield, Life Support's inert gas systems eliminate the potential for fuel-tank explosions when the birds come under enemy fire. This formidable force headquartered in Davenport, Iowa, has become the world leader in air-separation technology for military aircraft application. Founded by Bendix Aviation in 1951, Life Support has played critical, albeit changing, roles in the aerospace industry.

It has endured three parent companies while repeatedly revolutionizing the gas separation industry and steadily awed the military and medical oxygen communities to establish its reputation for excellence.

The company strength lies within its workforce of 300 extremely skilled employees, including some of the nation's finest mechanical, electrical and chemical engineers. Working in an integrated product-development team environment, they design, develop and refine the ever-evolving technology demanded by the world's finest armed forces.

To meet the challenges, professional and administrative staff work diligently to grow company markets and meet crucial military requirements, and highly skilled technicians produce Life Support's unique products to the finest of tolerance specifications imaginable. Their mission is critical, and their reputation remains impeccable.

Life Support holds numerous patents related to its three strategic business units — Life Support Products, Cryogenic Coolers and Medical Oxygen. These intellectual properties allow the company to dominate its markets while introducing successive and advanced generations of technology.

Life-Supporting Oxygen

Providing life-supporting oxygen systems to military aircraft is the core of operations. In fact, the company holds a 90 percent share of business in this highly specialized market. Each branch of the military depends on Life Support for customized applications of its product lines.

In addition to serving all branches of the U.S. military, Life Support's international business spans from Europe on the GR-7 Harrier aircraft in England to the C-27J transport in Italy. Military Air Forces in Brazil, Japan and Korea are valued customers as well.

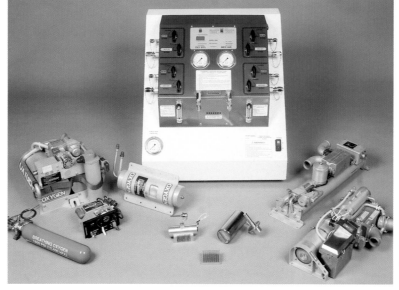

The company describes its military role as a mission to simplify logistics by virtually eliminating the ground-based support required for the aircraft oxygen system. For example, instead of having to fly back to a ship or base to refill oxygen tanks, Life Support technology, called on-board oxygen generating systems (OBOGS), allows prolonged flight time through self-generation of the life-sustaining gas. It is designed to automatically process pressurized air to produce a continuous supply of oxygen-enriched air.

An impressive array of military aircraft currently use Life Support OBOGS, including the AV-8 Harrier, F/A-18, F-14, T-45, F-15, F-16, V-22, T-6A, UH-60, A-4 and the F-5, as well as foreign aircraft such as the T/A-50, AMX, ALX and the PC-9.

This technology also is quickly becoming a new standard in oxygen and medical-grade air generation, eliminating the need to continually replace heavy pressurized oxygen cylinders at combat field hospitals during wartime and humanitarian missions.

Life Support's on-board inert gas generating systems (OBIGGS) are playing another essential role in the military by virtually eliminating low-flying aircraft casualties caused by ballistic threats to the aircraft's fuel tanks. An OBIGGS provides a continuous flow of nitrogen-enriched gas into aircraft fuel tanks, replacing the combustible fuel/air mixture in the tanks. The process significantly increases aircraft survivability and crewmember safety against fuel fires and fuel-related explosions, as well as environmental threats such as lightning and static discharge.

This technology is being produced for the AH-64 Apache helicopter, C17 Globemaster III, V-22 Osprey, AH-1Z and UH-1Y helicopters and the next generation Comanche helicopter.

Cryogenic Coolers

Another Life Support product line, miniature cryogenic coolers, is a key component of military infrared thermal imaging systems. This technology adds greater reliability and a tactical advantage to the military's night-vision community.

Applications for these cryocoolers include night sights and sophisticated weapon-targeting systems that allow soldiers to "own the night," enabling them the advantage of effectively seeing and fighting in the dark. These advanced infrared systems even allow soldiers to see through smoke.

An emerging application for cryocoolers mounts the cooler and the corresponding thermal imag-ing system on the skin of an aircraft. This system, called infrared countermeasures (IRCM) can detect an incoming heat-seeking missile and defeat it by using high-power laser technology to confuse it and send it off its course.

These advanced infrared systems also are highly utilized for weapon-system targeting from airborne platforms, ground-based armored vehicles and are emerging on naval weapon systems as well.

Medical Oxygen

In the medical oxygen market, Life Support was first to design an FDA-cleared cylinder-filling home-health-care oxygen concentrator. This product was derived from similar technology used to generate backup oxygen on board F-15s and Medevac helicopters.

Life Support recently introduced a new technology for the home oxygen market called a Ceramic Oxygen Generation System (COGS). This portable oxygen-generating device uses a ceramic membrane for air separation to produce oxygen on demand for customers in need of high-purity oxygen. This, like the company's military-related products, eliminates the logistics required to transport and refill oxygen tanks.

The company continually strives to adapt its core technologies for other markets. For example, cryogenic cooler technology is used in municipal and industrial markets to provide thermal images used for surveillance and process evaluation.

Breathing regulator technology is used to develop a closed circuit, self-contained breathing apparatus for personal protection in fire and hazardous material environments.

And, on-board oxygen-sensing technology evolved into oxygen monitors used in industrial-gas and health-care markets.

At left, Linear Cryogenic Coolers cool an infrared sensor enough to give it the sensitivity to detect the heat sources of this thermal image of Boeing's Chinook helicopter. The white coloring represents where there is the most heat; therefore, the engine is the whitest spot on the image. Below top, Engineer Scott Sehlin and Technician Craig Ross verify a new concept for Ceramic Oxygen Generation Systems in the research and development lab. Below bottom, Engineer Steve Jinks inspects a pneumatic boost pump prototype in the On Board Oxygen Generation System lab.

CARLETON LIFE SUPPORT SYSTEMS, INC.

2734 Hickory Grove Road
Davenport, Iowa 52804
(563) 383-6000
www.carletonls.com

Each year tens of thousands of residents and visitors flock to downtown for events celebrating the rich history of music in the community. Below, the River Music Experience, soon to be housed in downtown Davenport's historic Redstone building, will capture that energy and excitement year-round by providing a central destination where music lovers can enjoy local and regional talent, great food and changing exhibits about American Roots music.

Facing page: Top, kids have lots of options for fun because Davenport takes pride in delivering diverse environments throughout its 27 city-owned parks. Center, the riverfront of downtown Davenport is home to picturesque LeClaire Park, a haven for the city's mammoth music festivals and celebratory events. Bottom, a multi-million-dollar renovation is modernizing John O'Donnell Stadium while preserving its status as one of America's most beautiful historic ballparks.

the Mississippi River Bluffs Territory.

Davenport, Iowa, population 98,000-plus, is the regional beacon and hub of the metropolitan Quad-Cities, population 400,000, and the third largest city in the state. It is a place proud of its unique heritage at the crossroads of middle America and excited about a well-planned future that focuses on entrepreneurs, education, arts and entertainment.

The city's position along the banks of the mighty Mississippi River says so much about its significance. The working river and the region's fertile agricultural land first brought settlers to the area. These vital resources have spurred city growth since its incorporation in 1839.

Davenport was founded in 1836 by Antoine LeClaire, a lawyer and Indian interpreter, and named after his friend, Colonel George Davenport, a military provisioner and trader. It marked the beginning of a flurry of European immigrants, including a wealth of German and Irish who chose the city as a major settlement destination. Even today, the original honest, hard-driving work ethic brought by these immigrants has prevailed as one of the city's – and

the region's – most valuable assets.

Geographically defined by the unusual path of the Mississippi – the only place where the river runs from east to west – Davenporters like to say that the sun always shines on their city. Today, its rays are brighter than ever.

Go Davenport

Davenport is experiencing its greatest revitalization in more than 80 years, making it Iowa's most resurgent community. In addition to more than 50 economic development projects completed since 1993, more than $300 million is now being invested, and the results can be seen just about everywhere.

At the forefront of change is the strategic alignment of the City of Davenport, the Davenport Community Schools and DavenportOne, a chamber of commerce and business organization that fosters growth and development throughout the city. This joint initiative, called "The Go Davenport Partnership" is designed to build community momentum, reinforce a positive community image and pave the way for future success.

Davenport is a city doing big things. Its downtown is quickly

becoming a tourism and business mecca. The introduction of riverboat gambling, the renovation of the Adler Theatre and the creation of the RiverCenter convention facility sparked a wave of development a decade ago. Today, an unprecedented investment of public and private dollars has taken community development to a whole new level in anticipation of expanding business and tourism opportunities.

Construction is under way on major projects that show why Davenport is appealing to young professionals and families, including:

• The restoration of the historic Petersen building into The River Music Experience, a center that will capture the energy and excitement of music on the Mississippi through live performances and changing exhibits about the past, present and future of American Roots music.

• The River Music Sky Bridge, a spectacular pedestrian bridge providing an uninterrupted view of the Mississippi River and a safe connection for people between downtown and the riverfront.

• A renovated John O'Donnell stadium, a historic, scenic riverfront ballpark that enhances the city's minor league baseball experience and opens up opportunities for concerts and amateur sporting events.

- Mississippi Plaza, an upscale, six-story, multi-tenant office complex in the heart of downtown.
- The NewVentures Center, part of a new initiative that adds a new dimension to business development as a pipeline nurturing high-tech, ag-tech and other start-up companies.
- The Figge art museum, a nationally recognized cultural anchor in the region where people of all ages can meet, share and learn.
- Loft apartments in historic buildings, creating exciting new options for those seeking urban living experiences.

On the Upswing Everywhere

Davenport is the region's business and retail center, and the city's momentum continues in every direction from its downtown. Through establishment of an enterprise zone, incentives for business growth are helping non-retail operations purchase existing structures. Housing incentives are encouraging building and rehabilitation of single-family and multi-unit residential dwellings. And business development assistance attracts new construction or expansion for manufacturing, storage and offices.

In addition, Davenport's Eastern Iowa Industrial Center is ready, responsive and open for business with the construction of its first building, a 550,000 square-foot distribution center. The center is operated by Quad City Consolidation and Distribution through an exclusive contract with Deere and Co. To the east, the Iowa Research, Commerce and Technology Center is up and running with corporate headquarters for

Salzman International and Swiss Valley Farms.

Western Davenport is on the upswing, too. Once a burgeoning industrial area, the city is beginning environmental assessment and cleanup of old industrial properties, and plans are in place for quality improvements that will allow large corporations there to easily expand and new business to sprout. This effort is essential in the overall plan to make Davenport's River Drive a beautiful entrance to downtown. Farther north in western Davenport, the expansion of Locust Street and the extension of sewer service are creating a new area of prosperity.

As the city fills in its boundaries to the north, Davenport's 53rd Street Corridor has become one of the most significant commercial developments in the state, and it continues to expand its incredibly diverse blend of retail, entertainment and service businesses.

Transportation plays an essential role in strengthening the city's appeal. Four interstate highways, I-80, I-74, I-88 and I-280 serve the Quad-Cities, in addition to several U.S. and state highways, an international and a municipal airport and barge and rail transportation. Numerous truck terminals, distribution warehouses and industrial manufacturers are choosing this strategic geographic location that is within a day's drive of 34.7 million consumers and major metropolitan areas including Des Moines, Chicago, Indianapolis, Minneapolis, Kansas City, St. Louis and Milwaukee.

In Davenport and the entire Mississippi River Bend Region, recreational transportation is another flourishing commodity. Three national, one regional and a number of local recreational bike trails offer great choices for speeding up the exercise and slowing down the pace. On the Iowa side of the Quad-Cities, The American Discovery Trail runs from

Delaware to California; the Cody Trail traverses rural Iowa where Buffalo Bill once lived; Duck Creek Trail extends through Davenport and Bettendorf; the Mississippi River Trail links 10 states along the riverfront; and RiverWay enhances its winding riverside path with artwork, information kiosks and historical markers.

Then, of course, there's the beloved Channel Cat Water Taxi, crisscrossing the river with folks and their bikes so that kids of all ages can be connected with the unique diversity of several Quad-Cities' communities.

Where the Mississippi Celebrates

Adding to the high quality of life Davenporters enjoy is the city's national reputation for entertainment, the arts and espe-

THE GO DAVENPORT
PARTNERSHIP

Above, Davenport neighborhoods, like this one in McClellan Heights, are brimming with personality and amenities. Davenport's Fejervary Park is home to this aquatic center, one of two family waterparks new to Davenport.

DAVENPORT, IOWA

**226 West Fourth Street
Davenport, Iowa 52801
(563) 326-7711
www.cityofdavenportiowa.com**

DAVENPORTONE

**130 West Second Street
Davenport, Iowa 52801
(563) 322-1706
www.DavenportOne.com**

a winter home. And nothing beats a cup of hot chocolate while shivering through Davenport's giant Macy's-like balloon parade at the end of November, the kickoff for another mammoth regional favorite event, the Quad City Arts Festival of Trees.

The celebration continues into historic districts like the Village of East Davenport. Once an important logging community and Civil War encampment, the area along the Mississippi River is now a medley of boutique shops, restaurants and taverns. Unique festivals there highlight the likes of antique tractors, regional art and old-fashioned Christmas traditions.

The Power of Neighborhoods

When Davenporters lay their heads down to sleep, they feel safe, comfortable and happy. With an emphasis on preservation and enhancement, the mix of old and new neighborhoods is filled with rich culture and significance. From trendy downtown lofts in historic brick buildings to the resurrection of grand old mansions along Davenport's Gold Coast, community pride abounds as residents join together to preserve and highlight their designated neighborhoods' unique characteristics. Newcomers are always welcome to Davenport neighborhoods, and are often surprised by the open arms that greet them — another cherished Midwestern tradition.

In addition, new home growth in Davenport attracts both empty nesters and young professionals eager to build their own traditions. One example of planned new growth is Davenport's Prairie Heights, a new urbanism project that incorporates the best of older Midwestern architecture and craftsmanship and includes alleys, sidewalks and front porches to create charming streets that hearken back to the classic age of neigh-

cially river music. Many refer to Davenport as "the city where the Mississippi celebrates."

Each year tens of thousands of residents and visitors flock to downtown and to the riverfront for world-famous events such as the Mississippi Valley Blues Festival, the Bix Beiderbecke Memorial Jazz Festival and the *Quad-City Times Bix 7* run. Dozens of other festivals and events celebrate the community's rich musical history. With the development of The River City Music Experience in the historic downtown Redstone building, the celebration can continue even when the snow flies, although Davenporters always have been a hardy bunch. In the dead of winter, residents and visitors stand on the riverfront viewing hundreds of bald eagles that choose the area as

borhoods. Built into this model of quality development are neighborhood stores and parks within walking distance and environmental sustainability.

Momentum is Everywhere

More than 2,200 acres of parkland provide a plethora of recreational opportunities in 27 diverse environments. From historic Vander Veer Park, which is currently recreating its original historical attributes, to the modern Davenport Soccer Complex, with eight full-sized fields, parks are among our most prized possessions. The city also operates two public 18-hole and two nine-hole golf courses and several swimming pools, a children's zoo, ice-skating rinks, tennis courts and many parks with band shells that stay active with concerts and theater. Special programs abound for all ages.

Davenport is home to outstanding health care. Genesis Health System is ranked as one of the nation's Top 100 Integrated Health Systems, and includes the Heart Institute, a world-class center for a regional network of heart specialists. Also growing its presence is Trinity Regional Health System, which, in addition to clinics and services established in Davenport, is building a new state-of-the-art hospital, Trinity at Terrace Park in neighboring Bettendorf.

Davenport also is rich with educational and cultural opportunities. It is home to the Putnam Museum and IMAX® Theater, a library system second to none, St. Ambrose University, Palmer College of Chiropractic, Scott Community College, technical colleges, several private and parochial schools, and the city's Go Davenport partner in growth, the top-notch Davenport Community Schools.

Hᴵɢʜ EXPECTATIONS AND LOW CLASS SIZES, CUSTOMIZED CURRICULUM AND A CARING LEARNING ENVIRONMENT, $92 MILLION IN RECENT FACILITIES IMPROVEMENTS... THE DAVENPORT COMMUNITY SCHOOLS IS AN INTEGRAL PART OF THE SUCCESS OF THE DAVENPORT COMMUNITY.

The Davenport Community Schools has the resources of a large community with the small class sizes and hands on approach of a hometown school. With 30 schools serving the communities of Blue Grass, Buffalo, Davenport and Walcott, the Davenport Community Schools is resource-rich, blending student and family support programs with a wide range of curriculum to create a customized learning environment for all students.

High Expectations

In the Davenport Community Schools student achievement is the top priority. Authors, scholars, doctors, civic leaders... graduates of the Davenport Community Schools are a testament of the impact the institution has had on students and in the community. The schools are guided by articulated grade-level benchmarks to ensure that students are learning the skills they need for success in life and that programming in each grade is tailored to the needs of youth.

Customized Curriculum

Davenport Community Schools provides an extensive curriculum with courses and enrichment activities designed to keep the interest of each individual student. Well-rounded instruction starts in preschool with hands-on activities to encourage curiosity and independent discovery. Soft-light lamps, park benches in hallways, overstuffed reading chairs and lots of plants support a "brain friendly" environment for young learners. Vocal and instrumental music and use of technology in state-of-the-art classrooms and library media centers begins in elementary school. Intermediate schools allow students to expand their interests in the arts, foreign language and a wide range of extracurricular activities. School faculty understand the effect of adolescence on student learning styles. High school supports students with a variety of lifetime goals, with even more options within required course areas, expanded foreign language, advanced placement programs and even college-credit classes. Benchmarks and graduation requirements ensure that graduates are ready for the real world with career plans in place, ready to take their place in a post-secondary setting or the community.

Secure, Caring Environment

The Davenport Community Schools maintains a secure and caring learning environment for all students. The elementary environment is Concept-Based and Brain Compatible (CBBC,) with classrooms carefully designed to help minimize distractions and present subjects in ways that awaken the senses. Davenport's Skills for Life initiative teaches personal and social behaviors that help students interact positively and reach their full potential. The most tangible improvements to the learning environment, however, were through a voter-approved, one-cent sales tax, allowing $92 million in renovations over the last five years with more to come. Improvements include expanded learning environments; school and community collaborations, such as YMCAs built at local high schools; technology upgrades and energy-efficient building updates.

The bottom line... The Davenport Community Schools offers students a real-world education in a world-class learning environment.

DAVENPORT
COMMUNITY SCHOOLS

**1606 Brady Street
Davenport, Iowa 52803
(563) 336-5000
www.DavenportSchools.org**

THE GO DAVENPORT
PARTNERSHIP

DAVENPORT
COMMUNITY
SCHOOLS

Top left, elementary schools throughout Davenport embrace Concept-Based and Brain Compatible classrooms to help stimulate learning. Below left, Buffalo students, teachers and administrators celebrate the opening of the brand new Buffalo Elementary School in August 2002, one of an unprecedented series of building renovations throughout the Davenport Community Schools. Below, Davenport's West and Central high schools host the annual Great River Show Choir Competition at the Adler Theatre in downtown Davenport, attracting choirs and music lovers from six states.

WELCOME TO JOHN DEERE COUNTRY. AS HOME OF THE WORLD'S LEADING MANUFACTURER OF AGRICULTURAL AND FORESTRY EQUIPMENT, A MAJOR MANUFACTURER OF CONSTRUCTION EQUIPMENT AND A TOP PRODUCER OF EQUIPMENT FOR LAWN AND GROUNDS CARE, JOHN DEERE'S PRESENCE

is seen, felt and appreciated by the region's residents. In 1837, blacksmith John Deere developed the first commercially successful, self-cleaning steel plow in his one-man shop in Grand Detour, Ill. With its success, it wasn't long before manufacturing plows became the main focus of business, and in 1848, Deere selected Moline, Ill., for his expanding operation.

Just 70 miles south of his original shop, Deere chose wisely to take advantage of the water power and transportation offered by the Mississippi River. Today, with worldwide headquarters in Moline, John Deere has grown to employ 6,500 regional residents in Deere factories and offices at 27 locations throughout the Quad-City area. Globally, Deere & Company employs about 43,000 and does business in more than 160 countries.

Guided by its original core values — integrity, quality, innovation and commitment — Deere retains a stellar reputation in all four areas, which it considers an

asset of incalculable value. Deere continually strives to live up to these expectations, not just because it is good business, but because it is the right thing to do. Deere's goal, in short, is to build a business, and an investment, worthy of the quality products it makes and the uncommonly dedicated people who make them.

Pride of the Region

John Deere's presence throughout the Quad-Cities makes it the largest employer in the area. Deere & Company's World Headquarters

in Moline is one of the most celebrated headquarters buildings in the world. Designed by noted architect Eero Saarinen, the center's clean, practical lines and earth tones have won accolades from architectural authorities since its opening in 1964. Moline is also home to the John Deere Technology Center and factories that produce hydraulic cylinders, planters and seeders for the agricultural industry. In addition, administrative offices for Deere's construction and forestry group are in Moline, as are the

Top right, the John Deere Pavilion visitors' center on John Deere Commons in Moline opened in 1997. It is one of the top five tourist attractions in the state, hosting 250,000 visitors a year. The Commons complex is built on 20 acres of Deere-donated land where company founder John Deere established his first plow factory. Below, combines produced at John Deere Harvester Works, East Moline, are shipped around the world. Here, more than 1,000 combines start their journey to the Black Sea port of Illichevsk, Ukraine.

headquarters of the company's health care management services.

In neighboring East Moline, the company produces agricultural combines and front-end equipment and develops information systems for its dealer network.

In Davenport, Iowa, a mammoth John Deere facility produces backhoe loaders, motor graders, skidders and cabs for the construction industry. In Milan, Ill., another giant facility directs John Deere parts distribution for all divisions.

Outside the Quad-City-based operations, Deere & Company produces numerous products around the globe. Other Deere agricultural equipment includes tractors, harvesters, tillage tools, planters, hay equipment, cotton pickers and strippers, cultivators and various implements. For construction, public works, material-handling and forestry industries, additional major products include crawler dozers, tree harvesters and forwarders.

Deere manufactures all of its commercial and consumer equipment outside the Quad-Cities. It produces North America's broadest line of lawn and garden tractors, mowers and other outdoor power products for homeowners and commercial users.

Due in part to the success of its rapidly growing golf and turf

equipment line, Deere is the official equipment supplier for the PGA TOUR. A new market segment in this division, John Deere Landscapes, supplies irrigation equipment and nursery supplies to landscape service professionals across the U.S. The company also builds engines used in heavy equipment and provides equipment financing and leasing.

The Fun Side of John Deere

As a dedicated partner to Quad-Cities' economic development, John Deere plays a major role in improving quality of life. Its premier contribution of 20 acres of downtown Moline riverfront land, now transformed into John Deere Commons, is currently one of Illinois' top five tourist attractions. Here, the legend of John Deere lives on inside the sparkling John Deere Pavilion. This steel and glass visitors' center blends the nostalgia of old-fashioned farming equipment with the technology of computer simulation that fascinates visitors of all ages. More than just the history of a company, the pavilion shares the story of America by celebrating its heartland. The adjacent John Deere Store is a one-of-a-kind retail center, brimming with an eclectic and unique collection of American memorabilia featuring the renowned John Deere name

and trademark. Across the street, the John Deere Collectors Center is for enthusiasts interested in the nostalgia and legacy of John Deere and the collection of early John Deere tractors, equipment and memorabilia. There, visitors learn about restoration and collecting and can buy manuals for their own restoration projects.

Several historic sites complement the contemporary Commons project. They include Moline's Deere-Wiman House and Butterworth Center and the John Deere Historic Site in Grand Detour. Visitors can tour the majestic, historic homes situated atop hills overlooking the city and the Mississippi River. Charles Deere, John Deere's son, built both. In Grand Detour, visitors can explore the original homestead where John Deere created that first, and now famous, plow.

Among many other contributions to the area, John Deere donated land in Silvis, Ill., for what is now the PGA TOUR-owned-and-operated Tournament Players Club at Deere Run. There, Deere holds the title sponsorship of the John Deere Classic through 2010. The tournament attracts top PGA golfers and generates more than $1 million annually for local charities.

At top left, John Deere Series II Motor Graders on parade, built at the John Deere Davenport Works. In addition to motor graders, employees at the 2.2-million-square-foot facility build log skidders, four-wheel-drive loaders and cabs. At top right, the familiar John Deere green and yellow, shown here on this old tractor axle, is an important symbol of Deere & Company's quality products. Above, famed architect Eero Saarinen designed the home of Deere & Company's World Headquarters in Moline.

JOHN DEERE

DEERE & COMPANY

**One John Deere Place
Moline, Illinois 61265
(309) 765-8000
www.johndeere.com**

THERE IS A LOT OF PERSONALITY AND PRIDE THAT EVOLVES WITHIN A COMPANY THAT IS 150 YEARS OLD. DAVENPORT-BASED FIDLAR PRINTING COMPANY, THE OLDEST PRINTING PLANT IN IOWA AND A CORNERSTONE OF THE QUAD-CITIES' PRINTING COMMUNITY, HAS JUST THAT.

FIDLAR PRINTING COMPANY

**1515 East Kimberly Road
Davenport, Iowa 52807
(563) 386-2311
(800) 221-6834
www.fidlarprinting.com**

The Fidlar management team, top right, is building success through ideas, identity and pride. They are, from left, Ralph Anderson, chairman; Linda Rubey, vice president, director, client services; Michael Randone, president; and Bob Barstow, director-plant operations. Above, Frank Fidlar is shown at the company's 1915 location at Fourth and Perry streets, Davenport. Bottom right, a selection of the high-quality, brand-building marketing materials produced by Fidlar.

Working closely with clients to gain a comprehensive understanding of their branding requirements, Fidlar then sharpens its focus to infuse thought-provoking and innovative solutions that ensure client projects accomplish their intended goals.

It is what Fidlar Chairman Ralph Anderson only can describe as the "Fidlar Experience," and it allows the company and its employees their greatest opportunities to shine. Attention to detail, dependability, client comfort and on-time delivery all factor into each encounter with the company

Ideas. Identity. Pride.

To take the pain out of printing, Fidlar staff is big on ideas, identity and pride.

Ideas abound in the veteran sales force that looks to solve client challenges through a consultative approach. Client expectations are clearly communicated to and executed by a highly skilled workforce that lends its own brand of expertise to the process.

Maintaining and enhancing client branding **identities** are paramount to the quest for total quality. Fidlar staff is keen on meeting the standards each client insists upon, from client services to printing, fulfillment and distribution.

The **pride** Fidlar takes in accomplishing customer delight is apparent in the exceptional quality that comes off the press and in the award-winning work that exemplifies the company's capabilities.

Take, for instance, the die-cut, pop-up truck that actually sounds like a diesel engine. A printed piece? Yes. Or, count the Fidlar-

printed projects that, in any given year, win awards in the Quad Cities Advertising Federation ADDY® competition, the local contest that is part of the most prestigious advertising competition in the world. Fidlar shines.

Such accomplishments help the company retain long-term, loyal customers who depend on Fidlar to continually produce the best products possible. Moreover, Fidlar President Michael Randone insists, no matter how Fidlar touches a printing project, he knows clients will receive the best service and attention to detail possible.

Those who enjoy the "Fidlar Experience" develop strong, trusting relationships with their printer of choice. They know Fidlar is equipped to deliver to them every advantage possible.

Fidlar's niche is up-to-six-color, high-quality, commercial sheet-fed printing, although capabilities extend beyond that and include the world of digital communica-

tion, distribution and content management.

Community Values

True to its original 1854 philosophy of being a community player, Fidlar continues its commitment to charitable giving. In addition to ongoing efforts to better quality of life in the Quad-Cities, it takes on unique, heart-felt opportunities that tie directly to company capabilities.

"Home in the Midwest," a creative effort for the American Red Cross, comes straight off the Fidlar press. The company printed 5,000 sets of note cards featuring six beautiful illustrations by well-known local artists. The Red Cross delivered the cards to U.S. armed forces stationed overseas as part of its Treasures for Troops program.

I N 1869, THE FOUNDERS OF WHAT HAS BECOME GENESIS HEALTH SYSTEM OPENED ONE OF THE FIRST COMMUNITY HOSPITALS WEST OF THE MISSISSIPPI RIVER, BEGINNING A RICH HISTORY OF INNOVATION IN THE HEALTH CARE OF THE QUAD-CITIES REGION. TODAY, GENESIS CONTINUES TO GROW

Above, a Mercy Hospital nurse. Top right, the Genesis Heart Institute provides the focal point for a regional network of heart specialists. Below right, Genesis Health Group offers quality care at more than 30 offices in the bi-state area.

- building relationships with generations of families, contributing to the community, broadening services throughout the region and reaching new heights of excellence in health care. Its integrated system of health care services now spans the Quad-Cities metropolitan area and a 10-county region.

Genesis ranks as one of the nation's Top 100 Integrated Health Systems and has achieved regional and national firsts in groundbreaking research and surgery and earned some of the best patient satisfaction ratings in the country. Beyond its new technology, medical expansions and broadening network of providers, however, its greatest source of pride comes from its distinction as the Quad Cities' very own health system.

Genesis Health System, with more than 630 physicians and 5,000 employees, operates three full-service hospitals - Genesis Medical Center with two campuses in Davenport, Iowa; Illini Hospital in Silvis, Ill.; and DeWitt Community Hospital in DeWitt, Iowa. It also encompasses Genesis Health Group, the area's largest group of primary care practitioners; the Genesis Heart Institute, a focal point for a regional network of heart specialists; the region's only family practice residency program; four urgent-care centers; two long-term care facilities; an assisted-living center; a visiting nurse association and other diverse affiliates.

A 134-year journey

G enesis Health System's caring tradition spans 134 years. From expansions and technological innovation to the Sisters who worked tirelessly to care for

Courtesy of Flad & Assoc. Bob Harr@Hedrich Blessing

the poor to the generations of nurses and physicians who made the medical advancements unfold, its legacy is grounded in a mission to "provide compassionate, quality health services to all those in need."

Shaping the course of medicine

in the Quad-Cities, its institutions go back to the Catholic heritage of Mercy Hospital in 1869 and the Episcopalian roots of St. Luke's Hospital in 1895. Both began with similar traditions: The Episcopal Church and the Sisters of Mercy saw the need for com-

Oregionality

passionate ministry to the sick and dying in this community.

That religious and spiritual heritage continues as a foundation for the Quad-Cities' only locally owned and operated regional health care system. The evolution to bring cost-effective services to a broader, bi-state region began in 1993, resulting in the consolidation of St. Luke's and Mercy hospitals in 1994 to create Genesis Medical Center and then the subsequent birth of Genesis Health System.

It has continued with the addition of Illini and DeWitt Community Hospitals, a large physicians organization, a behavioral health services organization, the Genesis Heart Institute, the uniting of three visiting nurse associations, and a number of strategic partnerships and joint ventures.

Caring Relationships

There are many examples of how Genesis Health System has formed relationships and combined resources to meet communities' ever-changing health care needs.

It works hard to bring together health care experts to improve quality, unite precious health care resources and cultivate a wide network of providers.

The new Genesis Health Group - the uniting of River Valley Healthcare, Signature Physician Network and Genesis Medical Group - creates the largest network of primary care physicians in the region and offers more than 30 office sites in a seven-county area.

Likewise, a new partnership with Gastroenterology Associates, P.C., will bring new health care services to Bettendorf with Genesis at the Crow Valley campus, to be constructed at 18th Street and 53rd Avenue. The first phase will include office space for the physicians and an Outpatient

The new Family Room at Illini Hospital offers a homelike environment for moms and newborns.

Endoscopy procedure facility.

The new Genesis Occupational Health and Genesis Workplace Services focus more resources on the health care challenges faced by Quad City-area employers and offers the benefits of other programs of the Health System, including its nationally recognized Employee Assistance Program, Genesis Behavioral Resources and the multiple facilities of Genesis Medical Center's Outpatient Rehabilitation Program.

Compassion and Concern

Whether it's helping disadvantaged women receive prenatal care or substance abusers access treatment, Genesis Health System also builds relationships in the community that lend a hand to people at critical junctures in their lives.

Such initiatives include the new Edgerton Women's Health Center on the Genesis East campus, Quad City Safe Communities and the Quad Cities SafeKids Coalition and the CIRCLE of Hope residential substance abuse rehabilitation program at Illini Hospital.

Thanks to a new relationship with the Two Rivers YMCA in Moline, Illini has launched the PULSE, or People Utilizing Life-Saving Exercise, program – a medically supervised, individualized exercise program for cardiac patients and those at risk for heart disease.

Genesis Health System also continues to develop new and innovative partnerships to fill the community's health care gaps and

Right, Illini's Integrative Wellness Center of the Quad Cities in Moline offers a blend of traditional medicine with complementary therapies like acupuncture. Middle right, the Visiting Nurse Association of Genesis Health System gives patients medical support in the comfort of their homes. Bottom right, a pediatric nurse gives compassionate care and a story to a young patient at Illini Hospital.

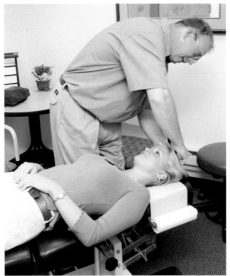

some of its most basic human needs, such as dental care, mammograms, health insurance for children and relief from life-threatening heat. It teams with the community to support such endeavors as the Quad-City Health Initiative, Hope Dental Clinic and Health Ministry Nursing.

Through strong ties to a number of Quad-City organizations, Genesis

Health System also works to give back to the community that has supported it for more than a century. Sponsorship support has included the Komen Quad-Cities Race for the Cure ®, Quad-City Times Bix 7, the YMCA, public-television station WQPT, Quad-City Arts, the Bettendorf Library, The Family Museum of Arts and Sciences, the American Heart Association, American Diabetes Association and the American Cancer Society.

Genesis Medical Center, Davenport, Iowa

The system's largest entity, Genesis Medical Center, provides 502 beds at two locations - East campus and West campus. Key service lines are cancer, physical medicine and rehabilitation, behavioral medicine, neurology and cardiology.

Over the past three years, more than $58 million in renovations on the East campus has brought a new Heart Institute, the focal point for a regional network of heart specialists; skywalk, parking ramp, BirthCenter, Neonatal Intensive Care Unit, Center for Breast Health, Medical Intensive Care Unit, new cardiac catheterization and electrophysiology labs; two new super surgical suites, and a new lobby and administrative offices.

Whether they're coming to the East campus for a heart procedure, recuperating in intensive care, giving birth to a child or visiting a loved one, Quad-Citians find their hospital experience is more family-focused and comfortable.

DeWitt Community Hospital, DeWitt, Iowa

DeWitt Community Hospital responds to a growing rural community by enhancing services for outlying areas north and west of the Quad-Cities.

Oregionality

People in DeWitt and surrounding communities enjoy access to physician specialists and advanced procedures close to home - thanks to provider relationships that bring services to their doors. The hospital's $7 million renovation and expansion has made it an even greater source of pride in the community.

Outreach clinics range from cataract surgery to cardiovascular care to podiatry. Other services include bone density screening, orthopedics, mental health, and a satellite lab and sleep clinic of the Genesis Sleep Disorders Center.

Westwing Place, DeWitt's 77-bed long-term care nursing unit, is a registered "Eden Alternative" facility, embracing the philosophy of using plants, animals and children to create an environment where elders live happily and comfortably.

Illini Health Services, Silvis, Ill.

Illini Health Services is an integrated network of health care providers and facilities serving health needs in a three-county area. Illini Hospital is a full-service, acute-care medical center, providing primary inpatient and outpatient care.

The Illini network is comprised of Illini Convenient Care, an urgent-care clinic; Illini Home Health Care; Illini Restorative Care Center, a skilled-care facility;

and Crosstown Square, an 85-unit assisted-living community; Illini Durable Medical Equipment; and the Integrative Wellness Center of the Quad Cities.

Illini's specialties include emergency and trauma, birthing services, orthopedic care, physical therapy and long-term care. After a

recent $6 million renovation, the hospital's obstetrics unit - called "The Family Room" - brings a comforting and homelike environment for moms and their newborns. Major technological upgrades have also brought a new CT scan and MRI machine to the hospital.

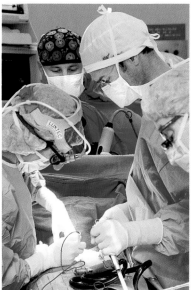

GENESIS
HEALTH SYSTEM

GENESIS HEALTH SYSTEM

**1227 East Rusholme Street
Davenport, Iowa 52803
(563) 421-2000
www.genesishealth.com**

HON INDUSTRIES Inc.
AND MUSCATINE, IOWA

Muscatine, Iowa, is home to HON INDUSTRIES headquarters and two of its subsidiaries, Allsteel, bottom left, and The HON Company, bottom right. Allsteel's #19™ Seating, right, has won several design awards for its incorporation of advanced ergonomic technology. The HON Company's award-winning Perpetual™ Seating, directly below, uses a unique frame design that automatically responds to the user for enhanced comfort and continual support.

In this flourishing, industry-friendly town of 23,000, HON INDUSTRIES is the community's largest employer and one of its greatest supporters.

Established here in 1944, HON INDUSTRIES provides products and solutions for home and workplace environments, and is one of the largest office furniture manufacturers in the United States. It is also the nation's leading manufacturer and marketer of gas- and wood-burning fireplaces, stoves, and hearth products.

Company brands – HON®, Allsteel®, Gunlocke®, Maxon™, Holga®, Heatilator®, Heat-N-Glo® and Quadra-Fire® – all hold leading positions in their markets, helping establish HON INDUSTRIES as a Fortune 1000 Company.

HON INDUSTRIES in Muscatine

Muscatine is the headquarters location for HON INDUSTRIES and two of its operating companies: The HON Company and Allsteel Inc.

The HON Company is a leading manufacturer and marketer of workplace solutions, including panel systems, seating, desks, storage files and tables. The HON brand offers a wide array of office solutions and outstanding customer service with a particular focus on small and medium-sized businesses. Operational excellence has made it an industry leader by providing quick delivery, fast service, and unparalleled quality.

Allsteel Inc. is a leader in the design, manufacture and marketing of workplace furniture that includes panel systems, desks, tables, storage products and seating. Allsteel targets the contract market, which is project-driven and design-oriented. Allsteel is known for high-quality, progressive workplace solutions.

Values-Based Strengths

HON INDUSTRIES is committed to maintaining its long-standing corporate values of integrity, financial soundness, and a culture of service and responsiveness. It has been recognized as one of the 400 Best Big Companies in America by *Forbes* magazine, and as one of America's Most Admired Companies by *Fortune* magazine.

The company credits its growth and success to the forward-thinking philosophy of its founders, C. Maxwell Stanley, Clem Hanson and H. Wood Miller. Before a product line was even crystallized, the three men first implemented a values-based business philosophy that clearly defined its intentions to treat employees, suppliers, customers, shareholders and communities with fairness, respect, honesty and integrity.

Staying true to those values, HON INDUSTRIES continues to support its workforce and the communities where they live with values-driven initiatives.

For example, HON INDUSTRIES employees are known as members. The term reflects more than a unique designation. It reflects – and drives – a unique level of commitment to the company's success throughout the

Oregionality

entire workforce. Now more than 8,000 strong throughout North America, members are encouraged to volunteer. As part of its long-standing beliefs, HON INDUS-TRIES plays an essential role in its community partnership with Muscatine through volunteer efforts by its members in civic, cultural, educational, environmental and governmental affairs and through financial support from the HON INDUSTRIES Charitable Foundation.

A Town Positioned for Excellence

Muscatine, a beautiful, quaint, historic river town on the banks of the Mississippi, shares a sense of pride with its business and community partners and is known for its family and community orientation.

Once called the "Pearl Button Capital of the World," based on buttons made from fresh water clams from the Mississippi, Muscatine today is known as "The Pearl of the Mississippi." From its century-old business district to its outstanding sports facilities and recreational areas, Muscatine is a true gem.

To improve the long-term vitality and quality of life for its residents, Muscatine stays keenly focused on developing and maintaining community amenities.

Its excellent municipal power, water and communication utilities, beautiful parks, and a strong school system are testimonies to its dedication to creating an attractive and cooperative climate for business, industry and families.

In addition to HON INDUS-TRIES, Muscatine also is home to myriad large, medium and small companies known nationally and internationally for their products. Major employers include Stanley Group, Grain Processing Corp./ Kent Feeds; H.J. Heinz, Bandag, Monsanto, BT Prime Mover, and Musco Lighting.

Above, the Muscatine Soccer Complex was recognized by the National Turfgrass Managers Association as the "best soccer facility" in 2002. This 41-acre complex features eight full-sized, state-of-the-art, premiere soccer fields. Below, historic downtown Muscatine is known for charming shops filled with antiques, fine furniture, outstanding art and unique specialty items.

HON INDUSTRIES INC.
P.O. Box 1109
Muscatine, Iowa 52761-0071
(563) 264-7400
www.honi.com

CITY OF MUSCATINE
City Hall
215 Sycamore Street
Muscatine, Iowa 52761
(563) 264-1550
http://ci.muscatine.ia.us/

WITH THE SIMPLE TURN OF A FAUCET, THE WATER FLOWS – SAFE, CLEAN AND ALWAYS AVAILABLE. IN THE IOWA QUAD-CITIES AND CLINTON, IOWA, THERE'S A REASON SUCH HIGH-QUALITY WATER SERVICE IS OFTEN TAKEN FOR GRANTED. IT'S BECAUSE NO ONE KNOWS WATER LIKE IOWA AMERICAN WATER.

Above, Iowa American's Middle Road Tank and Booster Station are designed to create an aesthetically pleasing, park-like setting for neighbors. At right, construction workers install some of the first water mains in the Iowa Quad Cities on River Drive in Davenport.

At the helm of these communities' water systems for more than 125 years, Iowa American Water's expertise and vast resources in water treatment, pumping and distribution make it a model utility.

In fact, in 2001, the company's Quad-Cities District became the first water utility in Iowa to be awarded the Partnership for Safe Water program's Director's Award in recognition of its achievements in high-quality drinking water and continual improvements.

The program, a voluntary initiative of the U.S. Environmental Protection Agency (EPA) and other water organizations, is comprised of only 248 water utilities from across the country that work together to enhance drinking water quality and operational excellence in water treatment. Within the group and Iowa, Iowa American Water stands out as an industry leader.

Building the Tradition

I t was 1873 when the local company's early leaders had the foresight to construct a then-modern water treatment plant on the shore of the Mississippi River, just a mile upstream from Davenport's Government Bridge.

Today, at that very same site, Iowa American continues to build its tradition of quality using the most sophisticated tools technology has to offer, coupled with water research and management skills gained through its long history of investor ownership.

A Mighty Resource

N ot surprisingly, Iowa American Water utilizes one of the area's greatest assets, the Mississippi River, as its water source in the Iowa Quad-Cities.

On an average day, 17 million gallons of water reach more than 130,000 Iowa Quad-City residents, and 3 million gallons serve more than 30,000 residents in the Clinton area. In October 2003, Iowa American will welcome more than 1,000 new customers in LeClaire, Iowa.

Several large projects have improved the company's ability to achieve high standards:

• In the last decade, Iowa American has invested almost $35 million in major treatment plant improvement projects that enhance its water clarification processes, filtration techniques, chemical-feed methods, equipment and storage. All of these projects have been designed with flood protection in mind.

• A $2.3-million distribution tank and pump station in Bettendorf, Iowa, now provides additional water storage to satisfy growing service demands and improve fire protection flows in the community.

• A $2.4-million, seven-mile pipeline to interconnect Iowa American's Quad-Cities District with LeClaire, is slated for completion in October 2003.

In its Clinton District:

• More than $500,000 has been invested in recent years on several large-diameter pipeline projects undertaken to greatly enhance fire flows and pressures to several of Clinton's largest industries, as well as to reinforce the western portion of the Clinton distribution system.

• A $184,000 renovation to the building structure, aeration unit and chemical feed systems of one of the seven deep wells in Clinton was accomplished to address safety and reliability issues.

Iowa American Water works hard at ensuring customers receive the highest levels of service at reasonable costs. Conveniences include centralized billing, an automatic bill-paying service, local payment centers and emergency service 24 hours a day, seven days a week.

And, because reliable water

service is the lifeblood of business and industry, Iowa American is poised for growth and development that creates jobs. The company's contribution to the communities it serves is achieved through vast technical expertise, managerial experience and ability to invest financially. It is also based on its commitment to high standards of environmental and social performance. Its affiliations provide mass purchasing power that result in savings on items including fire hydrants, valves, chemicals, pipes and meters.

Iowa American's ability to attract the best research talent in the world has helped establish top-notch regional laboratories equipped with the latest water-quality technology, including a national research and testing laboratory in Belleville, Ill., regarded as one of the finest in the country.

What Makes Water Pure?

Water for the Iowa Quad-Cities is taken from the Mississippi River and treated in Iowa American's state-of-the-art East River Station treatment facility. The high-tech water treatment plant uses some of the best equipment and technology available to the water industry. In fact, more than three decades ago, Iowa American pioneered the use of granular activated carbon filtration, a process that, even today, only a small number of water utilities have put into place. The U.S. EPA calls it one of the most effective treatment technologies for the removal of organic chemicals, such as farm pesticides and industrial wastes. It is also highly effective in eliminating many taste and odor problems.

In the Quad-Cities, Iowa American uses a multiple treatment barrier approach that includes

screening of debris, chemical treatment, clarification, filtration, corrosion control, fluoridation and disinfection. State-certified water professionals are on duty around the clock, every day, to assure drinking water that is better than government standards require.

In the Clinton District, the water source is seven deep wells in four well fields in the Clinton area. The wells average 2,200 feet in depth and supply water of excellent quality requiring only minimal treatment.

The Clinton District obtains its water from the Cambrian-Ordovician and Cambrian aquifers. Chlorine is added to the water supply to assure microbiological quality, and fluoride is added to promote strong teeth. A phosphate compound is added to treat the small amount of iron that occurs naturally in well water and to minimize corrosion. Due to the depth and confining beds of rock above the aquifers, Clinton's source of supply has excellent protection from potential sources of contamination.

In fact, Iowa American was recently commended by the U.S. Centers for Disease Control and Prevention for providing the benefit of fluoridation, considered one of the 10 most important public health measures of the 20th century, to its customers for more than 50 years.

In all of its service areas, Iowa American monitors water quality continuously and gathers and tests samples throughout the treatment process, at well and pump stations and throughout the distribution system, including public buildings, schools, hospitals, apartment complexes and private residences.

Iowa American Water's long tradition of quality service in eastern Iowa proves its commitment to its customers and communities. Customers can take that cool, clean drink from the tap for granted because Iowa American Water doesn't. Now that's a liquid asset!

At left, Iowa American employees are pictured at the company's new customer-friendly Operations Center on Grand Avenue in Davenport that opened in 2003. Below, company employees at the Davenport, top, and Clinton, bottom, plants work diligently to ensure safe water is delivered to all residents in its two districts. Below left, water quality specialists monitor water quality.

Iowa American Water

IOWA AMERICAN WATER

Quad-Cities District
5201 Grand Avenue
Davenport, Iowa 52807

Clinton District
2020 Manufacturing Lane
Clinton, Iowa 52732

www.iawater.com

Toll free: (866) 641-2108
(24 hours/7 days a week)

ISLE OF CAPRI AND RHYTHM CITY CASINOS

R IVERBOAT GAMING WAS A CHALLENGE BERNARD GOLDSTEIN COULDN'T RESIST. WHEN THE IOWA LEGISLATURE CONSIDERED THIS FIRST-IN-THE-NATION PROPOSAL, THE RETIRED BARGE COMPANY OWNER WAS FRONT AND CENTER, LOBBYING HARD FOR PASSAGE. IN 1989, IOWA GAVE THE NEW INDUSTRY

Above, the Quad-Cities' own Bernard Goldstein, the Father of Riverboat Gambling. At right, visitors to Rhythm City are greeted with the sounds and sights of the casino's musical theme. Below right, guests relax in the spacious and friendly lobby of the Isle of Capri Hotel.

its official stamp of approval, and Goldstein put away his golf clubs and went back to work.

The appeal was too great to pass up. Goldstein's family owned Iowa's only barge line with riverboat captains and engineers who knew the Upper Mississippi like nobody else and, to boot, they had a stretch of property on the Bettendorf, Iowa, riverfront that was ideally located for such a venture.

Fast-forward to 2003. Bernard Goldstein, often referred to as the Father of Riverboat Gaming, now navigates the Isle of Capri Casinos, Inc., as chairman of the board and chief executive officer. The company operates in Colorado, Iowa, Louisiana, Mississippi, Missouri and at Pompano Harness Track Park Racing in Florida. It is one of the top 10 publicly held gaming companies in the U.S., generating more than $1 billion in revenue.

In addition, the Isle of Capri has signed a Heads of Terms agreement with a partnership including the City of Coventry, England, to install a casino in their new soccer stadium/exhibition hall complex that should be under construction in 2004, and open in 2005. And on August 14, 2003, the Isle received a gaming license from the Commonwealth of the Bahamas for a license to operate a casino at the Our Lucaya Resort in Freeport on Grand Bahamas Island.

Because of the Isle's extensive experience in multiple gaming jurisdictions, it is one of the most seasoned companies in the industry and, along with it, one of the most popular.

Today, it continues its quest for acquisitions. Nevertheless, Goldstein's heart and soul remain in the Quad-Cities, where the

company operates two Iowa casino properties – the Isle of Capri in Bettendorf and Rhythm City in Davenport.

Winning Customers, Employees

A t both Quad-City entities, which are located just four miles apart, guests enjoy a superior entertainment experience in a fun, clean, secure and friendly environment. Employees benefit, too, through formalized training, competitive compensation and benefits and a fun working atmosphere that encourages long and rewarding careers. In fact, Isle casinos have one of the lowest turnover rates in the industry. Employees are empowered through skills and tools to give the best service possible to guests. The two casinos employ about 1,500, and staff take strong active roles in local chambers of commerce, tourism organizations, civic clubs, local charitable organizations and patronization of local businesses and services.

The company appreciates its employees, calling them the "face of the Isle of Capri casinos." Management highly values their dedication to the company mission — "to be the best for its guests, its employees, its communities and its investors … not the biggest, but the best."

Isle Style

W hereas Davenport's Rhythm City carries a music-based brand, Bettendorf's Isle of Capri epitomizes the company's unique brand as a tropical island paradise. The two differing themes are a result of a marketing strategy that provides visitors two entirely different, first-class gaming atmospheres.

The tropical-themed Isle of Capri is actually a resort-style complex that includes the floating casino, a hotel, convention and meeting facilities, restaurants, shops and live entertainment. It is one of the Midwest's largest riverboat casinos with more than 1,100

slot machines and 36 hot table games operating 24 hours a day.

The Isle hotel features 256 spacious rooms and 36 luxury suites, a heated pool and fitness center, a 17,000-sq.-ft. meeting/event center and a 500-space parking garage. Three restaurants serve up plenty of variety: Farraddays', specializing in steak and seafood complemented by exotic worldly dishes served in a casual, gourmet atmosphere; Calypsos Buffet, an all-you-can-eat breakfast, lunch and seafood dinner extravaganza; and Tradewinds Marketplace, offering delicious Chicago-style hotdogs, burgers and more. Guests enjoy live, on-site entertainment at the Caribbean Showroom and Penguins Comedy Club. The Isle's most recent addition, a 50-slip marina, welcomes pleasure boaters as well as vessels as large as the visiting Delta Queen and American Queen cruise boats.

Where Rhythm Rules

Rhythm City provides an excellent contrast to the Isle by delivering fun and excitement through a timeless music theme. It features more than 1,000 slot machines and 19 table games, two music-themed restaurants, and a historic 121-room hotel setting, the Blackhawk, which offers a relaxing and elegant change of pace after the excitement of the casino.

The Hit Parade Buffet serves up tasty temptations for breakfast, lunch and dinner and features Midwest favorites such as barbecue ribs, prime rib and peel-and-eat shrimp. Rock Around the Clock, a 1950s-style diner, serves blue-plate specials and classic fountain-style desserts 24 hours a day. Play n Eat service delivers nostalgic drive-in favorites right to players' slot machines or table games.

Branding Success

Isle of Capri Casinos, Inc., unique approach to standardize procedures in marketing and operations – called Islestylezation – plays a key role in enabling the company to serve its guests and has contributed to the remarkable advances and sound financial performance of the company. This smart working philosophy truly has been the foundation upon which Isle properties have grown.

Bernard Goldstein is delighted to see the growing success of his two hometown casino properties, his confident, friendly employees and the Quad-City community. His goal to make the area a regular destination for visitors keeps him busy and satisfied. And although Iowa is the only state that requires riverboat casino operators to share a percentage of profits with the communities in which boats are located, he is more than pleased to comply. Each year, more than $6 million in contributions goes to community nonprofits to spearhead projects from arts and economic development to education and health and human services.

Above, the Rhythm City Casino complex on the Mississippi River in Davenport, Iowa. Below, the resort-style Isle of Capri Casino and Hotel in Bettendorf, Iowa.

ISLE OF CAPRI CASINO & HOTEL
**1777 Isle Parkway
Bettendorf, Iowa 52722
(563) 441-7000**

RHYTHM CITY CASINO
**101 West River Drive
Davenport, Iowa 52801
(563) 328-8000
www.theisleofcapricasino.com**

*E*LEVATORS AND ESCALATORS – THEY ARE THE HEARTS THAT KEEP BUILDINGS ALIVE. WITHOUT THEM, THE CIRCULATION OF PEOPLE AND GOODS IN OUR CITIES WOULD SLOW TO A STANDSTILL. THEY, AND THE PEOPLE WHO INSTALL AND SERVICE THEM, KEEP US ON THE MOVE.

KONE INC.

**One KONE Court
Moline, Illinois 61265
(800) 956-KONE (5663)
www.kone.com**

At right, the KONE tower soars above the skyline along the banks of the Mississippi River, delivering an awe-inspiring welcome to the heart of the Quad-Cities. Below, The KONE ECO3000™ escalator, manufactured in Coal Valley, Ill., is engineered to achieve new levels of efficiency, space savings, reliability and aesthetics. Bottom, KONE MonoSpace®, the company's premier gearless product, is setting industry standards as the first elevator in the world that does not require a machine room.

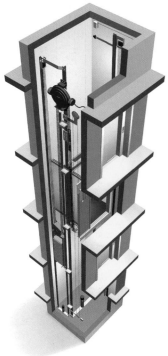

An essential player in the world of vertical transportation conducts its business from Moline, Ill. KONE Inc., the North American headquarters of the global KONE Corporation, provides complete solutions for the installation, modernization and maintenance of elevators, escalators and autowalks.

A Towering Presence

Since its transformation from locally owned Montgomery Elevator, founded in 1892, to KONE in 1994, the company has grown to include more than 50 offices and 200 sub-offices across the country. KONE employs about 4,500 in the U.S. and about 500 in the Quad-City area.

With its prominent presence along the banks of the Mississippi River next to the Interstate 74 Bridge, people are naturally curious about the company, its tower and even its name.

KONE – pronounced kō-nāy and always spelled with capital letters – is a Finnish word for machine. Its corporate headquarters are in Helsinki, Finland. Its two divisions are KONE Elevators & Escalators and KONE Material Handling. KONE operations span the globe, throughout Europe, North America, Asia and Australia and employ almost 36,000. It is the third largest vertical transportation company in the world.

In Moline, the KONE test tower and research facility is a community landmark equivalent in height to an 18-story building. Inside the tower, engineers research, develop and test KONE's elevator modernization products. On top of the tower, a lower floor serves as a testing room, and the upper level is a conference room

with the finest panoramic view in the Quad-Cities. The tower's famed Christmas tree has been a holiday tradition since 1966 and is hoisted annually from the ground by a crane that is permanently installed at the top of the tower.

At one time, the sprawling riverfront facility beneath the test tower manufactured elevators. Today, it houses KONE's administrative headquarters for North America, and the manufacturing of elevators is in McKinney, Texas. KONE builds escalators in the Quad-Cities at its Coal Valley, Ill., factory. In addition, Moline is home to the company's North American 24-hour call center, spare-parts distributions center and the Quad-Cities Sales and Service Branch.

Dedicated to Excellence

KONE expresses its strong brand values – innovation, dedication and reliability – visually, verbally and in behavior across the organization to all its audiences.

For example, the company's revolutionary KONE EcoDisc® hoisting unit has changed the way the world thinks about elevators by setting industry benchmarks for technology and environmental friendliness. KONE EcoDisc® improves space efficiencies, reduces energy consumption, extends product life and requires no oil. KONE EcoDisc® technology powers all of KONE's EcoSystem® products, including KONE MonoSpace®, the world's first successful machine-roomless elevator. KONE ECO3000™ escalators are raising global standards for space savings, style, safety, environmental friendliness and sound design.

Keeping people and goods on the move is a lofty responsibility, and KONE takes that to heart. With a workforce second to none, the company dedicates itself to optimizing product performance, harnessing new technologies and going the extra mile – always.

Oregionality

I T'S NOT UNCOMMON FOR RESIDENTS IN THE REGION TO KNOW THAT THE DAVENPORT PLANT OF LAFARGE NORTH AMERICA IS ACTUALLY LOCATED IN BUFFALO, IOWA. IT IS, HOWEVER, UNCOMMON FOR THEM TO KNOW EXACTLY WHAT LAFARGE PRODUCES. SIMPLY PUT, THE COMPANY MAKES CEMENT —

At right, Lafarge quarries limestone, an important natural resource for making cement, at the Buffalo plant site. Below, Lafarge product is used to create a new highway bed on the Rock River bridge in Moline.

not concrete, as many mistakenly label it.

What's the difference? Well, cement is to concrete as flour is to bread. It is the principle strength-giving and property-controlling agent of its end product, concrete.

The Perfect Mix

While production of cement is essential to perfecting the mix that creates concrete, the Davenport Plant also describes its entire operation as "The Perfect Mix" of innovative *people,* quality *products* and a beautiful *place.*

Between 72 members of the Brotherhood of Boilermakers, Lodge D-6, and 38 staff employees, the Lafarge Davenport Plant annually produces more than a million tons of fine powder

cement. Used to create building materials for everything from concrete sidewalks, homes and roads to bridges, dams and skyscrapers, cement is second only to water as the most consumed substance on earth. It was 1927 when Dewey Portland built the plant in the tiny town of Buffalo. In 1962, Martin Marietta purchased the facility, followed by Cementia in 1983. It became a Lafarge North America property in 1991.

Positioned strategically between the Mississippi River, a major rail system and America's busiest Interstate highways, Lafarge has easy access to barge, rail and bulk trucks. The plant is a leader in market share in its 150-mile region and also serves a good portion of the Minneapolis/St. Paul area.

The Davenport Plant is one of 20 Lafarge cement-making facilities across the U.S. and Canada. Combined, Lafarge is the largest supplier of cement and concrete in North America. Globally, Lafarge North America is part of the Lafarge Group, the world leader in building materials. It is active on five continents. The group holds

leading positions in all four of its divisions — cement, aggregates and concrete, roofing and gypsum.

At the Davenport Plant, customers are at the very core of Lafarge's strategy to listen, respond and deliver the finest Portland, slag and blended cement products. Each product carries its own virtues:

• Portland cement is a high-quality, cost-effective, basic building material used in virtually all forms of construction.

• Slag cement is a finely ground hydraulic cement called NewCem® that provides flexibility in concrete proportioning, resistance to chemical reactions, superior strength potential and improved workability.

• Blended cements are a series of products used in high-performance applications where enhanced strength and durability properties are required, such as bridges, underwater structures and industrial flooding.

An additional asset is the site's open-pit limestone quarry. Limestone makes up 80 percent of cement; the other 20 percent being iron, silica and aluminum.

Although Lafarge experts have determined the pit's life span is another 50-plus years, a plan is already in place to reclaim the property as a natural park-like environment featuring native plants, recreation, a marsh and a lake.

Innovative People and Solutions

Lafarge continually reinvests in the operation to improve processes and efficiencies. Today, it is state of the art, with remote controls built into the flow to ensure employee safety, environmental compliance and quality products.

In addition to its quarry and processing capabilities, an on-site concrete laboratory provides technical benefits for customers. Along with conducting standardized compliance testing of its cement products, the lab can translate specific customer concerns for concrete setting times and strengths into data.

Lafarge manufacturing experts then use the information to create solutions to challenges customers may have when using Lafarge products.

In an industry where blasting rock and heavy machinery use is an everyday occurrence, Lafarge is serious about employee safety. In fact, its comprehensive safety program was the model for Lafarge North America's corporate safety

program. At the time of this book's publication, the plant has achieved more than four years without a lost-time accident.

The plant also is highly proactive in caring for the environment. The facility's emissions are controlled to keep the surrounding air clean.

Lafarge's ambient air-monitoring station measures emissions and dust in real time — not just at the Lafarge plant, but also across the entire area. The manufacturing process is continuously controlled to maintain emissions well below the allowable level.

Reducing energy consumption is another priority at Lafarge. The Lafarge Group has a corporate initiative to voluntarily reduce CO_2 emissions, and in 2000, the Davenport Plant installed a cement conveyor-belt system that has vastly reduced its energy needs.

Caring for Community

Teams of Lafarge employees contribute to the vitality of the community's land and water resources.

You'll find employees working to keep the shores of the Mississippi River clean though participation in Living Lands And Waters and the Adopt A Mississippi River Mile programs.

The company continually searches for opportunities to recycle by-products from other industries, and each year the Davenport Plant collects tons of materials from businesses for reuse in the cement-making process in place of raw materials.

Lafarge employees also actively participate in a number of other cultural, health and educational programs in the community, including Junior Achievement, Camp Abe Lincoln and United Way of the Quad Cities.

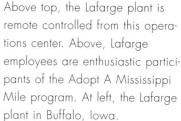

Above top, the Lafarge plant is remote controlled from this operations center. Above, Lafarge employees are enthusiastic participants of the Adopt A Mississippi Mile program. At left, the Lafarge plant in Buffalo, Iowa.

LAFARGE NORTH AMERICA RIVER REGION

Davenport Plant
301 East Front Street
Buffalo, Iowa 52728
(563) 323-2751
www.lafargenorthamerica.com

WITH A PASSION FOR LOCAL NEWSPAPERS AND STRONG BELIEF IN THEIR FUTURE, DAVENPORT, IOWA-BASED LEE ENTERPRISES REIGNS AS THE 12TH LARGEST NEWSPAPER COMPANY IN THE UNITED STATES AND THE PREMIER GROUP SERVING MID-SIZE COMMUNITIES. A.W. LEE FOUNDED LEE IN

Right, Mary Junck, chairman, president and chief executive officer, leads Lee, the premier company operating newspapers in mid-sized markets. Below, this photo, taken on the New York Stock Exchange (NYSE) trading floor in 1978, marked the beginning of Lee trading on the Big Board under the ticker symbol "LEE." Taking part in the ceremonies were, from left, William Batten, chairman of the New York Stock Exchange (NYSE), Lloyd Schermer, Lee CEO from 1973-91, and NYSE Specialist Robert Shaw.

1890 in Ottumwa, Iowa, and most of today's Lee properties trace their beginnings to the mid-1800s. Among Lee alumni: Mark Twain, Willa Cather and Thornton Wilder.

Its intriguing story speaks of a reporter who died with George Custer at the Battle of the Little Bighorn and ownership of the first newspaper in the world to be produced totally by computer.

Throughout its rich history, Lee Enterprises has been a model of determined leadership, innovation and high ideals.

Lee's current holdings in 2003 include:

• 44 daily newspapers in 18 states
• 175 weekly newspapers, shoppers and specialty publications
• An expanding array of online services

Lee The Man

The company is named for Alfred Wilson Lee, an ambitious young man who entered the University of Iowa at age 13 and took his first newspaper job at the *Muscatine Journal* about 1880. Lee's father, John, was head bookkeeper there, and the owner and publisher, John Mahin, was married to Lee's sister.

By 1890, Lee decided to become a publisher himself, working with local investors to take charge of the *Courier* in Ottumwa, Iowa.

He later conceived of the idea for a group of newspapers, each controlled by his family and associates, yet each with local ownership, each an independent corporation and each as local as the city hall or the town pump.

Lee The National Leader

Mary Junck, a veteran newspaper administrator, leads today's Lee Enterprises. The company remains active on the acquisition front, with an emphasis on strengthening positions in essential markets by clustering dailies and weeklies.

Its workforce numbers more than 6,700 employees in 18 states, and its newspaper circulation is more than 1.1 million daily and 1.2 million on Sunday. Additionally, it reaches hundreds of thousands more through other publications.

Although the company also once

owned network-affiliated and satellite television stations, Lee decided to return to its roots in 2002 – producing publications with paper and ink.

With its focus in place, Lee now concentrates on its top priorities: growing revenue creatively and rapidly; improving readership and circulation; emphasizing strong local news; building its online future; and exercising careful cost control.

As the parent company, Lee is comfortable taking a back seat to its individual newspapers. And by design, the company keeps a low profile.

Quality Starts Success Cycle

Quality journalism is central to Lee's success. Year after year, Lee newspapers garner top awards with significant local journalism that draws more readers. By drawing more readers through local news, advertisers gain further reach, and it is their support that drives the financial success of Lee newspapers.

In turn, that financial success powers Lee's news engines, allowing them to expand statehouse bureaus, develop online news and attract top-notch journalists. That strengthened local journalism starts the Lee cycle all over again. At the end of 2003, Lee Enterprises entities in this Mississippi River Bend

Region include:
• Davenport/Quad-Cities publications: *Quad-City Times, Bettendorf News, Quad-City Business Journal, On the River, Wheels For You, Thrifty Nickel* and *Work For You.*
• Muscatine area publications: *Muscatine Journal, Classic Images, Films of the Golden Age* and *The Post.*

In addition to *Quad-City Times* and *Muscatine Journal* Web sites, regional online services include Townnews.com in Moline, Ill. Regional commercial printing services include Hawkeye Printing and Trico Communications in Davenport. Lee publications are also found in California, Idaho, Illinois, Indiana, Iowa, Kentucky, Minnesota, Montana, Nebraska, New York, North Dakota, Oregon, Pennsylvania, South Carolina, South Dakota, Washington, Wisconsin and Wyoming.

The year 2003 marked Lee Enterprises' 25th anniversary on the New York Stock Exchange, where it enjoys the distinction as one of only two such companies with Quad-Cities' headquarters. The other is Moline-based Deere & Company.

Lee's community role is also a very important aspect of its focus. As opinion leaders, Lee's newspapers strive to interact with readers and help improve communities. They sponsor and participate in

numerous charitable organizations and community events, and employees serve on various community boards and committees.

New Headquarters Under Way

Lee Enterprises remains committed to downtown Davenport and plans to move its national headquarters to the top two floors of a $14.3 million office building being developed by Ryan Companies Inc. The building is scheduled for completion in May 2004.

Lee chose downtown Davenport because it wanted to remain a part of the excitement and momentum of the area's economic development initiatives.

Above, the new home of Lee Enterprises opens in May 2004 in this $14.3 million structure at West Second and Harrison streets in Davenport. Below, shown in the press room of the *Quad-City Times*, are Lee Enterprise officers, from left, Brian Kardell, vice president for production and chief information officer; Kevin Mowbray, vice president for sales and marketing; Greg Schermer, vice president for interactive media; Carl Schmidt, vice president, chief financial officer and treasurer; Mary Junck, chairman, president and chief executive officer; Greg Veon, vice president for publishing; Michael Phelps, vice president for publishing and publisher of the *Quad-City Times*; Vytenis Kuraitis, vice president for human resources; and Nancy Green, vice president for circulation. Officers not shown include David Stoeffler, vice president for news; and James Hopson and John VanStrydonck, vice presidents for publishing.

LEE ENTERPRISES

215 North Main Street
Davenport, Iowa 52801
(563) 383-2100
www.lee.net

MIDLAND INFORMATION RESOURCES

Below, at their spacious Davenport headquarters building, is the Midland Information Resources executive team, from left, John Klein, Liz Terrill, Gene Blanc, Randy Epkes, Craig Woodard, Mary Gehrls, Michelle Bates and Tom Sheehan. Above, print-on-demand employees display some of the company's array of projects that are customized to the individual.

that industry is efficiency. Never saying never, thinking outside the box and always asking, "What if?" is the philosophy that helps keep this burgeoning company at the forefront of innovation. Merging technologies, streamlining practices, building better systems and creating fresh solutions for its worldwide clientele reflect the substantial commitment in capital and human resources Midland makes to exceed customer expectations.

Midland Information Resources, the parent company of both Midland Press Corporation and Transcend Software, Inc., is a leading-edge provider of highly unique services that encompass content management, digital printing, fulfillment and distribution solutions.

CEO Gene Blanc knew when he built Midland as a traditional printing company in 1982 that technology would inevitably change his world. Forward thinking moved his team of employees to push the envelope and create affordable print-on-demand — a process that could be compared to what is commonly known as just-in-time manufacturing.

For example, Midland's digital

printing systems now deliver a company's manual of technical information to meet the specific needs of one service mechanic, and a different set of technical information for another. Or maybe a person prefers the information on CD-ROM. Can do — customized to the individual — one at a time. However, print-on-demand was just the beginning of Midland's transformation. By surrounding itself with excellent people, Midland continued to build complex information resource services.

Midland Press Corporation

T his half of the company focuses on the digital printing and distribution side of information management solutions. From the print-on-demand programs mentioned above to more straightforward printing-to-inventory options, Midland Press specializes in getting clients' valuable company information into the hands of the people who

need it — when they need it.

To achieve its goals, the company has collaborated with some of the biggest names in the industry to develop and implement leading-edge technology in electronic file management, digital platemaking, short-run traditional printing, digital printing, and one-off book printing and distribution.

Housing more digital print engines in one facility than virtually any other printer in the country, Midland's people, technology and solutions are setting the bar in the print-on-demand arenas. Midland occupies more than 85,000 square feet of state-

of-the-art technical, manufacturing and warehousing facilities specifically designed to meet tomorrow's electronic print and information distribution needs. It operates 24 hours a day, seven days a week, to ensure quick-turn capabilities and maximum utilization of its equipment and systems.

Transcend Software Inc.

The ability to manage content successfully — to create it, to ensure its conformity and consistency and to deliver it according to focused, personalized needs — is an increasingly challenging task for organizations that expect to reap the benefits of competently managing their business information.

Enter Transcend Software, the technology arm of Midland that specializes in developing content management solutions. Through a unique blend of technology, software development and consulting services, the company partners

with customers to develop online business strategies customized to fit individual communication needs.

As a certified reseller and system integrator for the Stellent suite of products, and a systems integrator for both Microsoft and Adobe product lines, Transcend helps clients develop solutions that control and expedite the delivery of information critical to a daily business operation.

The company is committed to building scalable and cost-effective information management and distribution strategies for departments, business units or entire enterprises.

Solutions can be developed for Internet, intranet, extranet or client server environments, and can be made available for distribution through a variety of mediums, including print, CD-ROM, DVD or web publishing.

It's All About the People

It's a complicated business to operate an organization like Midland Information Resources. The management team believes that the key to success is balancing the needs of its five partners — employees, customers, shareholders, suppliers and the community.

Blanc believes his employees, with their creative and entrepreneurial spirits, are the true assets of Midland. He is committed to the 200-plus employee team and

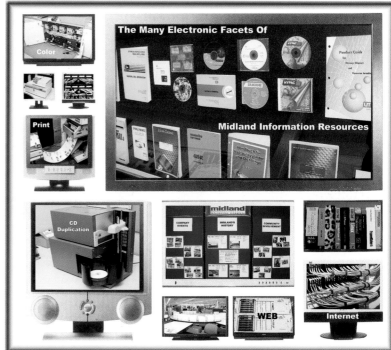

provides for their well-being with safe, comfortable, ergonomically correct working conditions, flexibility in work responsibilities, recognition for volunteer efforts that help build a better community and positive support of family life. The company even employs four full-time trainers to give staff opportunities to enhance their skills.

Not surprisingly, for the second year in a row, Midland Information Resources has been nationally recognized with the "Best of the Best" award in the "Best Workplace in America" competition sponsored by the Master Printers of America.

Community Caring, Sharing

The company's philosophy that centers on people and fulfilling their needs spills over into the Quad-Cities' community. While Blanc himself is known as a tireless volunteer and role model, he delights in the fact that his employees are also enthusiastic volunteers. To him, it goes hand in hand with character building and leading a fulfilled personal and work life.

Above left, Transcend Software trainers provide customers with comprehensive web-based instruction. Above, a product sampling of the many facets of information distribution. Below left, four full-time, on-site trainers provide Midland employees many opportunities to advance their skills.

MIDLAND INFORMATION RESOURCES

5440 Corporate Park Drive
Davenport, Iowa 52807
(563) 359-3696
www.midlandcorp.com

H ELPING OTHERS IN TIMES OF HARDSHIP. THAT'S WHAT JOSEPH CULLEN ROOT SET OUT TO DO IN 1883 WHEN HE FOUNDED MODERN WOODMEN OF AMERICA. HE WANTED TO ELIMINATE THE FINANCIAL BURDEN FAMILIES FACED WHEN A BREADWINNER DIES.

And he wanted Modern Woodmen members to stand by one another through good times and bad. With their actions, they brought to life the expression "neighbors helping neighbors."

Today, Modern Woodmen's nationwide network of 1,100 representatives and 460 home office staff members continues to carry out Root's vision.

Modern Woodmen offers fraternal financial services. It was established in 1 ns, Iowa, in 1883, and has been based in Rock Island, Ill., since 1897. As a fraternal, not-for-profit membership organization, it goes beyond providing financial products.

The organization also offers additional member benefits for families, along with social and volunteer service programs that help members help their communities.

Helping members achieve quality of life is at the core of everything that is Modern Woodmen of America. It is one of the country's largest fraternal organizations, touching the lives of more than 750,000 members nationwide.

Financial Security for Families

M odern Woodmen's high-quality portfolio includes permanent life insurance, term life insurance, annuities, retirement plan options, mutual funds* and brokerage services*.

Additional types of insurance products available, offered in most states and through other carriers, include major medical, disability income and long-term care. At year-end 2002, life insurance in force totaled $28.5 billion, and total assets reached nearly $5.6 billion.

Through MWABank**, a wholly owned subsidiary of Modern Woodmen of America, members and others can establish Certificates of Deposit, and checking and savings accounts, receive consumer loans and obtain credit cards.

Fraternal Benefits

A s a fraternal organization, Modern Woodmen touches lives with more than financial products. Members also have access to many other benefits, as well as social and volunteer opportunities. Members may qualify for college scholarships or Medic Alert membership. Modern Woodmen's Fraternal Aid Fund provides financial assistance for premium payments in times of financial hardship.

Its Grief Assistance program provides a special booklet to help beneficiaries cope with life after the death of a loved one. An Orphan Benefit gives support to member children who lose their parents. Newborn Benefits assist parents of children in poor health. Accelerated Benefits provide living benefits for the terminally ill. The organization offers a library of free informative medical booklets covering various health topics. A Child Identification program and Prescription Drug Discount program also benefit member families.

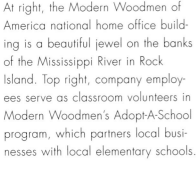

At right, the Modern Woodmen of America national home office building is a beautiful jewel on the banks of the Mississippi River in Rock Island. Top right, company employees serve as classroom volunteers in Modern Woodmen's Adopt-A-School program, which partners local businesses with local elementary schools.

Always Focused on Families

Modern Woodmen's founder envisioned an organization that would "provide wholesome social activities and character building." To this end, Modern Woodmen established a lodge system of local chapters known as camps. Camp members of the late 1800s enjoyed picnics, parades, baseball games and monthly meetings.

Today's fraternal programs focus on the social needs of modern-day families. More than 2,200 camps improve quality of life in communities across America through social gatherings and meals, fund-raising events and hands-on improvement projects. Fund-raising projects alone contribute more than $5 million to community projects nationwide each year.

For children across the nation, more than 700 Modern Woodmen Youth Service Clubs provide social, educational, patriotic and volunteer service activities for young members. Children learn the importance of sharing with others, caring for those in need and giving back to their communities, and they have a lot of fun, too.

Additionally, nearly one-million children benefit from Modern Woodmen Youth Educational Programs each year. Schools, home-school associations and youth groups can receive a free program guide and complete kit of materials on topics including ecology awareness, bicycle safety, safety awareness, public speaking, creative writing and a safety-conscious autumn celebration.

Fraternalism Begins at Home

At the Modern Woodmen home office in Rock Island, employees emulate the core values of fraternalism through myriad opportunities to volunteer.

Employees are encouraged to develop their volunteer spirits in programs like Adopt-A-School, a community program spearheaded by Modern Woodmen. The organization grants employee volunteers one hour off work each week to serve as tutors and helpers in classrooms at Rock Island's Lincoln Elementary. Nine other companies have joined the organization in this community endeavor, adopting other Rock Island elementary schools.

Many Modern Woodmen employees and their families volunteer at and participate in the Modern Woodmen-sponsored Bald Eagle Days, a fun and educational event celebrating the migrating eagles that roost in the Quad-Cities' area each winter.

These and numerous other Modern Woodmen sponsorships and activities incorporate the organization's family-focused philosophy.

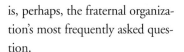

What's in a Name?

What does Modern Woodmen mean? It

is, perhaps, the fraternal organization's most frequently asked question.

The name "Modern Woodmen of America" honors the pioneering woodmen who cleared the forests to build new homes, communities and security for their families.

Founder Joseph Cullen Root harnessed that spirit and created Modern Woodmen to clear away financial difficulties for all families with life insurance. The phrase "of America" signifies members' patriotic spirit.

Bottom left, Modern Woodmen's nationwide force of representatives places a high priority on helping families plan for the unexpected, as well as the future. Leading the fraternal financial services organization into the 21st century is President Clyde C. Shoeck, left.

MODERN WOODMEN OF AMERICA

MODERN WOODMEN OF AMERICA
1701 1st Avenue
Rock Island, Illinois 61201
(309) 786-6481
www.modern-woodmen.org

ONSANTO IN MUSCATINE, IOWA, IS IN THE BUSINESS OF HELPING PRODUCE FOOD FOR THE WORLD'S POPULATION IN A SAFE, ENVIRONMENTALLY SUSTAINABLE WAY. SOME MAY SAY THAT'S A TOUGH ROW TO HOE, BUT HERE, IT IS QUITE THE OPPOSITE. MAKING A ROW EASIER FOR A FARMER

to hoe is precisely its mission.

Since establishing itself in 1961 as an employer of choice for more than 500 of the area's residents, the plant has become a model of flexibility and proven capabilities, a factor that is key for Monsanto now and in the future.

Beginning first as a producer of anhydrous ammonia, the plant progressed quickly into the herbicide arena in 1964 with the invention of Randox®.

Many generations of herbicides later, the Muscatine facility stands as one of global Monsanto's premier producers of Roundup®, the world's best-selling and environmentally safest herbicide on the market. It also produces many other selective herbicides for corn, soybeans, rice and wheat.

Globally, Monsanto is a leading provider of agricultural products and integrated solutions for farmers. In addition to Muscatine's capabilities, the company produces leading seed brands and provides farmers and other seed companies with biotechnology traits for insect protection and herbicide tolerance.

On its own, Monsanto Muscatine serves a vast market, serving farmers in the upper Midwest, the Plains states, the western United States and Canada.

At right, the process of making herbicide starts here in one of the many chemical silos located at Monsanto in Muscatine. Below top, Ron Dunker is behind the scenes running the remote controlled A-Unit from a plant control room. Below bottom, James Clark prepares Roundup® for distribution.

Earning the Freedom to Operate

Safety, community involvement, environmental stewardship, open dialogue and diversity all are key values at the plant and pillars of the global Monsanto pledge. Through ongoing programs in these areas, Monsanto in Muscatine demonstrates a deeply held respect for its employees, community and other stakeholders.

Attention to these values allows Monsanto the "Freedom to Operate," according to Muscatine Plant Manager Oscar Berryman. By this, he means the facility must continually earn its place as a best-practice manufacturer that protects the safety of all who encounter its operations, the community and the environment.

At the root of the company's success are its loyal employees. Their dedication to retaining the plant's status as a world-class manufacturing facility is paramount to long-term viability and success.

The plant encourages a forward-thinking climate by incorporating many components related to worker satisfaction and comfort, such as ergonomically correct equipment, educational opportunities, safety training and stock options. By doing so, employees have embraced the importance of their roles to improve agricultural productivity and reduce farming costs.

Monsanto's excellent employee safety record speaks for itself. The plant is a Voluntary Protection Program Star plant, which means it meets the strict safety standards of the U.S. Occupational Safety and Health Administration (OSHA).

Technology, of course, also has influenced work processes at Muscatine. The plant is highly automated and includes computer systems that control all manufacturing processes. The automation allows for larger projects, as well as more sound environmental emission control and energy savings.

Producing the World's Finest

The invention of Roundup®, a non-residual knockdown herbicide that controls more than 300 common weeds and is environmentally friendly, was an incredible breakthrough for the company.

Monsanto was keen on the fact that once its protected patent was lifted by government regulations in 2000, the competition would rush to emulate the Roundup® formula, and they did. Meanwhile, Monsanto kept its sights on differentiating itself in quality, reliability and performance.

To remain a leading force in this highly competitive market, the plant quadrupled its production capacity between 1997 and 2002, placing it in a sound position for asset utilization and optimization.

It also established itself as one of the few agricultural chemical manufacturers to hold ISO 9001 status, a universal system that measures product quality and customer satisfaction, awarding certification only to companies that can prove consistency in both areas.

Always on the cutting edge, the company continues to search for more opportunities to deliver benefits to smaller farmers and larger growers, while continually addressing environmental issues.

The latest breakthroughs in the Muscatine laboratory include a new formulation called Roundup Weather Max® transorb technology. This herbicide absorbs and adheres to plants better than any other herbicides, making it more adaptable to varying weather conditions, such as cold snaps.

Another challenge is perfecting Roundup Ready® products, a new generation of herbicides that complement biotech seed that has herbicide-resistant traits built into its composition. This allows farmers to practice conservation tillage and no-till methods, which prevent erosion, maintain moisture in the soil, lower farming costs, and deliver higher-quality and better yields.

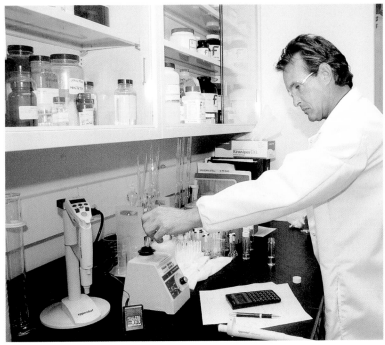

Steward of the Environment

However, all at the Muscatine plant is not about staying ahead of the competition. Monsanto is highly sensitive to environmental protection.

It is a charter member of the National Environmental Performance Track of the U.S. Environmental Protection Agency. This program credits manufacturing plants that excel in environmental performance, take extra steps to reduce and prevent pollution and demonstrate they are good neighbors to the people in their communities.

The plant's attention to the environment extends beyond monitoring emissions. For example, in concert with neighboring Mid-American Energy and the Louisa Ecological Advisory Committee, Monsanto developed Big Sand Mound Nature Preserve. This 510 acre nature habitat is home to more than 650 species, including the Illinois Mud Turtle, considered almost endangered in 1978. The boundaries of the preserve establish critical habitat for the healthy survival of this population.

Muscatine plant employees also have restored undeveloped plant land back to its natural prairie state, planted hundreds of cedar and oak trees along an aging tree line and established a butterfly garden near the plant entrance for all to enjoy.

Above top, Chemist Joe Dies performs quality control testing in the Monsanto lab. Above bottom, John Gomes prepares packaging for shipment of Monsanto Roundup® products. At left, A class tours the sand prairie on 65 acres of Monsanto property that employees restored to native grasses and wildflowers.

MONSANTO

2500 Wiggens Road
Muscatine, Iowa 52761
(563) 263-0093
www.monsanto.com

MUSCATINE JOURNAL

**301 East Third Street
Muscatine, Iowa 52761
(563) 263-2331**

Below top, Mark Twain once said of Muscatine, "I remember Muscatine for its sunsets. I have never seen any on either side of the ocean that equaled them." Below bottom, no city in the country boasted as many button factories as Muscatine, once known as the "Pearl Button Capital of the World." Below right, The *Muscatine Journal's* location since 1919 at the corner of Cedar and Third Streets, in historical downtown Muscatine.

The name was changed to *Muscatine Journal* in 1849 when the town's name also was changed.

John Mahin and Alfred W. Lee, both legendary in the history of Lee Enterprises, worked at the *Journal*. Mahin, and father Jacob, purchased the *Journal* in 1853. Lee purchased the newspaper in 1903. Mahin, in control of the *Journal* in the late 1800s, was the center of a dangerous confrontation over liquor. He staunchly opposed the liquor traffic and in 1893 his home was severely damaged by a bomb.

The *Journal* also was the place Mark Twain had some of his first writings published in 1853 because his brother worked at the *Journal*.

In the early 1900s the *Journal* was caught in the middle of a bitter labor dispute in the fresh-water pearl button industry. Twice in those years, troops were sent to the city.

The *Journal* moved into its current building in 1919. Today, it houses the combined operations of the *Journal* and the Muscatine Trading *Post*, a weekly shopper also owned by Lee Enterprises. Printing for the Muscatine operations is performed at the *Quad-City Times* in Davenport, Iowa. The *Journal* and *Post* have about 40 full-time staff members.

The *Journal* is part of the Quad-Cities strategic business unit for Lee Enterprises. Its role is to provide as much local news coverage as possible, while giving readers both local and regional advertising information. And, because of the city's large manufacturing base, a constant influx of new workers and executives brings many new faces to the community each year. These new faces are not native to the region, and, therefore, also look to the *Journal* to provide coverage of state and regional news and sports.

Almost 95% percent of adults in the Muscatine area read either the *Journal* or *Post* during the week, making these publications the dominant news and advertising medium in the market.

Dating as far back as the 1800s, Muscatine has made its place along the Mississippi River without a lot of fanfare. Originally known as Bloomington, the city changed its name to Muscatine in 1850 in hopes of stopping its mail from being delivered to Bloomington communities in Illinois and Indiana.

Lumber and button making dominated Muscatine in the late 1800s and early 1900s. As the industrial revolution spread across the country, Muscatine soon became home to some of the top industries of the day in Iowa. Today, that claim still can be made.

Muscatine can boast HON INDUSTRIES, Monsanto, Bandag, Heinz, GPC/Kent Feeds, Musco Sports Lighting and IPSCO Steel that all have large manufacturing and production facilities.

The riverfront is undergoing a multimillion-dollar renovation to include a walking trail, playground, new boat dock and marina and meeting facility. Muscatine's eight-field soccer complex hosts the state

high school soccer tournaments each spring and its 20-plus baseball/softball field facility hosts tournaments all summer. And, because of their high concentration of top companies, Muscatine and Muscatine County have one of the highest per capita income rates in the state.

Interesting facts

• The *Journal* was among the first newspapers to publish Twain's writings, albeit not under the Mark Twain byline. In the 1850s, Samuel Clemens' brother worked at the *Journal*. Still a teenager, Sam Clemens wrote five "dispatches" to the *Journal* that were published between 1853 and 1855. They were brief descriptions of sights and sounds from his travels across the Midwest and to the East Coast. Three were signed with a "W," possibly a shorthand signature for one of his early pen names. The other two are signed S.L.C. for Samuel Langhorne Clemens.

• In the late 1800s, *Journal* editor John Mahin's opposition to liquor trafficking put the newspaper in the center of a firestorm. The Mahin home was bombed, resulting in severe damage to the house. The family, asleep upstairs, managed to escape.

Oregionality

To say that Norcross Safety Products L.L.C. (NSP) grew its business from the ground up might sound trivial, but it is actually quite literal. Founded in Rock Island as Servus Rubber in 1921, the business began with manufacturing rubber boots and tennis

NORCROSS SAFETY PRODUCTS

**1136 Second Street
Rock Island, Illinois 61201
(800) 777-9021
www.nspusa.com**

footwear. Fast-forward 74 years to the company's transition to become Norcross Safety Products in 1995. Strategic change has propelled the company from footwear alone into a complete line of personal protective equipment (PPE) from, well, toe-to-head.

In fact, NSP is the fifth largest manufacturer of PPE in the world, holds a 90-percent market share for fire-fighting footwear and, as of 2002, is the last surviving rubber safety footwear manufacturer in the U.S. What is PPE? If it protects the human body from injury, it is likely to be in the company's product lineup. NSP encompasses three subsidiary companies, each with their own specialties in the protection industry. North Safety Products dominates eye, ear, hand, respiratory and fall protection; Total Fire Group is the leader in personal protection for the fire-

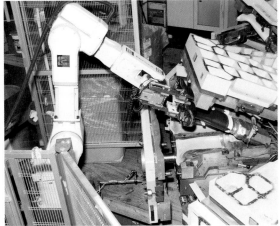

fighter; and W.H. Salisbury & Co. is the foremost manufacturer of protective equipment required by electric utility workers.

Leading the Pack

At the heart of the Rock Island headquarters operations is the manufacture of waterproof protective footwear for all divisions of the conglomerate.

Hand-labor-intensive processes, virtually the same used since the 1920s, produce high-quality rubber protective footwear for consumer outdoor, as well as industrial and occupational markets.

In contrast, Rock Island headquarters, which is ISO 9001 certified, produces PVC injection-molded footwear using state-of-the-

art technology, complete with robots that remove and trim product. Rock Island is also headquarters for consumer retailing, which includes protective products for outdoor sporting, lawn and garden, and farm and ranch markets. In all, NSP employs 4,000 people worldwide with 350 in Rock Island. Operations spread throughout the world in New Hampshire, Rhode Island, South Carolina, Quebec, Ontario, the Netherlands and South Africa.

NSP continues its aggressive acquisition strategy into an even broader realm of PPE. Current Rock Island brands include Northerner, Servus, XTRATUF, Ranger, North, and the company's

most recently acquired brand, The Original Muck Boot Co.

Tradition of Quality

Through the years, NSP has served an impressive number of high-profile accounts. The U.S. Armed Forces were priority clients in the 1940s and '50s, when Gene Autry, "The Singing Cowboy," served as company spokesperson. Most recently, the NSP plant in Nashua, N.H. provided chemical/biological warfare protective footwear for the Iraqi Freedom campaign. NSP operates a footwear manufacturing plant in China in order to compete in price-sensitive markets. Yet the majority of protective footwear sold by NSP is made domestically – and "made in the USA" is still a very important strategy in the company's future plans.

Contrasting technologies — a robot that removes and trims PVC injection-molded footwear, far left, and good-old hand work that perfects high-quality rubber footwear, top left — both are integral methods of production at the Norcross headquarters factory in Rock Island. Also at left are two groups of products representing the toe-to-head personal protective equipment solutions offered by the company. Current brands include those shown below.

IN THE UNIVERSE OF PLUMBING, HEATING AND AIR CONDITIONING, THE WORD "BEAUTIFUL" RARELY COMES TO ONE'S MIND. HOWEVER, FOR ENGINEERS AT NORTHWEST MECHANICAL, THE AREA'S PREMIER MECHANICAL CONTRACTING COMPANY, BEHIND THE SCIENCE OF THE TRADE LIES TRUE ART.

At right, Project Manager Tom Luethye, standing, and Estimator Dennis Harden review working drawings for an upcoming project. Below, the art of mechanical design is reflected in this attractive sculpture-like piping.

Proper design, construction and installation of the winding, twisting, turning pipes, ducts and tubes that create the infrastructure of all buildings could just as easily be interpreted as industrial sculpture as it is raw power.

Every client's need is unique; every design requires new vision. Mechanical contracting melds science and art to bring life and comfort to a building's occupants.

Changing With the Times

Terry Hester owns and operates Northwest Mechanical. He purchased the business in 1983 from the James Hintze family, which owned the company for 60 years.

Family tradition endures, with Terry's son Greg Hester preparing to take over the reigns from his father in 2005, while all else in the business has evolved with technological and industrial growth. Since 1983, business volume has increased more than 30 times. Staff has skyrocketed from six to 140. Moreover, "A pipe is no longer a pipe," according to Hester.

Rather, industry demands now require such specialized components as food-grade, high-purity and ammonia piping, new processes such as orbital welding and technologically advanced instruments including automatic temperature controls.

With success dependent on staying ahead of technical trends, Northwest invests heavily in leading-edge equipment, college- and trade-educated employees, and continuous training for all employees.

The professional staff drives success by teaming skills and energies, and Hester takes pride in the company's developing a reputation as "the place" to work. An office staff of 30 supports professional engineers, designers and project managers whose singular desire is to provide solidly designed systems, quality installation, a strong guarantee and professional service throughout the life of each product.

As a union-organized shop, Northwest is a strong advocate of accomplished craft people. Hester depends on Union Local 25 Plumbers and Pipefitters to provide the skill levels he insists upon, and praises the local union for its outstanding commitment to apprentice training and continued education for journeymen.

Formula for Success

Hiring the absolute best candidates for the many positions in mechanical contracting has been a strategy that has propelled the company's pursuit for total quality in all of its competencies.

Company philosophy dictates that employees work hard, have a good time and celebrate their successes. Hester believes that placing the right personality within the Northwest team accomplishes those mandates, reduces stress and improves performance. It also has translated into very little staff

turnover. The company has developed long-standing working relationships with community leaders by giving clients the best possible experience from start to finish and beyond through maintenance and service.

High-profile clients include Deere & Company, 3M, Quad-City Times, St. Ambrose University, MidAmerican Energy, the Davenport, Pleasant Valley and East Moline school districts, and both Genesis and Trinity health systems.

Northwest differentiates itself by continuing to enter specialized markets with highly technical piping systems. One growing specialty, hospital mechanical construction and service, requires such processes as medical gas installation and has grown to include 10 hospital clients.

At Your Service

Northwest is a full-line mechanical contractor with three operating divisions.

The Mechanical Construction Division is an industry leader providing mechanical "design and construct" commercial, institutional and industrial mechanical projects. On-staff mechanical engineers and designers work with the latest Auto CAD and QuickPen CAD software to provide state-of-the art working drawings.

Using the industry's latest scheduling software, project managers ensure owner and construction manager deadlines are met. This division also operates a high-tech, efficient union-label pipe-fabricating plant.

The Mechanical Service Division focuses on commercial and institutional heating, ventilating, air conditioning and building controls. It operates under the national franchise corporation, LINC Service, which develops maintenance programs that recognize a broad spectrum of mechanical systems requirements. The technology ensures proper scheduling of preventive maintenance on a regular basis. Individual equipment profiles for each client assure longer equipment life cycles, efficient operating conditions and improved air-quality comfort conditions.

The Plumbing and Service Division is one of the oldest and largest residential and small commercial plumbing, heating and air conditioning services companies in the area, providing 24 hour service, 365 days a year. From its centrally located headquarters in Davenport, Northwest Mechanical serves the entire western-Illinois/eastern-Iowa region.

From repairing a home faucet and overhauling a temperature control unit to installing a sophisticated piping system in a plant, the Northwest team is dedicated to quality workmanship and outstanding performance.

Near left, Terry Hester, standing, and son Greg Hester lead Northwest Mechanical's progressive, can-do staff. Below left, Northwest operates its own efficient union-label pipe fabricating shop. Above left, a chilled water-cooling system is meticulously placed atop the MidAmerican Energy office building in Davenport. Directly below, a service employee performs preventive maintenance to ensure longer equipment life, efficient operating conditions and improved air quality.

NORTHWEST
MECHANICAL, INC.

NORTHWEST MECHANICAL, INC.

5885 Tremont Avenue
Davenport, Iowa 52807
(563) 391-1344
www.northwestmech.com

P.O. Box 332
Pleasant Valley, Iowa 52767
(563) 332-5550
www.pleasval.k12.ia.us

T HE PLEASANT VALLEY COMMUNITY SCHOOL DISTRICT OFFERS A UNIQUE BLEND OF SUBURBAN AND RURAL LIVING. THIS SETTING, ALONG WITH A STRONG COMMITMENT TO EDUCATIONAL EXCELLENCE, CREATES AN IDEAL ENVIRONMENT TO EDUCATE STUDENTS. SINCE 1962, THE DISTRICT HAS

prided itself in fostering outstanding achievement for all students with an emphasis on continuous improvement, small class size, and meeting the needs of individual students.

As a result of the focus on student achievement, the district is consistently able to recognize and celebrate many accomplishments – standardized test scores far exceeding the state average, high degrees of parent and student satisfaction, outstanding ACT scores, post-secondary enrollment exceeding 90 percent and a notable number of National Merit scholars honored each year.

Preparing Students

T he Pleasant Valley School District serves the educational needs of about 3,200 students in four K-6 elementary schools, one 7-8 junior high and one 9-12 high school. The district's comprehensive and well-articulated plan for instruction is designed to prepare students to maximize their full learning potential as they grow toward productive careers and citizenship. From a strong emphasis on the acquisition of the basic skills associated with reading, writing and mathematics at the elementary level, students progress to the more varied and self-selected course opportunities available at the secondary level.

Providing Unique Opportunities

T he district provides unique learning opportunities at each level. At the elementary, this includes a balanced approach to teaching literacy, a focus on mathematical problem solving and hands-on science opportunities taught by science specialists. At the junior high, this encompasses a strong literacy component with a double period of language arts, exploratory opportunities through orientation classes and character development through the adviser-advisee program. The unique offerings at the high school incorporate service learning opportunities for all students, the provision of eighth period resource to support academic assistance and enrichment for all students and the availability of multiple Advanced Placement course offerings.

The well-rounded preparation of Pleasant Valley students is further strengthened by excellent opportunities in athletics, the fine arts, service organizations, and a wide variety of clubs and activities.

Through its extensive community involvement, well-planned use of resources, and committed parents, students and teachers, the Pleasant Valley Community School District continues to strive to provide its students an innovative education with a personal touch.

Above right, Pleasant Valley High School features state-of-the-art technology in its classrooms. Students, right, get invaluable, hands-on experience. Below, Riverdale Heights Elementary is one of four elementary schools serving the Pleasant Valley school district.

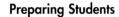

WHEREAS *OREGIONALITY*, THE BOOK, IS A SINGULAR, COMPREHENSIVE ACCOUNT OF LIFE IN THE MISSISSIPPI RIVER BEND REGION, IT IS THE FULL-TIME, YEAR-ROUND DUTY OF THE QUAD CITIES CONVENTION AND VISITORS BUREAU (QCCVB) TO SHOWCASE THE EVER-CHANGING,

QUAD CITIES CONVENTION AND VISITORS BUREAU

Mississippi Valley Welcome Center 900 Eagle Ridge Road Exit 306, Interstate 80 and U.S. Highway 67 LeClaire, Iowa

Moline Depot Welcome Center 2021 River Drive Moline, Illinois

Union Station Welcome Center 102 S. Harrison St., Davenport, Iowa

563-322-3911 800-747-7800 www.visitquadcities.com

always-growing attractions of the area to almost one million visitors a year. The bureau staff is a vibrant, enthusiastic group of professionals who market and sell the Quad-Cities' area as one complete destination. With three visitors' centers – Union Station at 102 S. Harrison St., Davenport, Iowa; the Moline Depot at 2021 River Drive, Moline, Ill.; and its showpiece, the Mississippi Valley Welcome Center at 900 Eagle Ridge Road, LeClaire, Iowa – the bureau is the official welcome wagon for all who travel to enjoy the region's famous Midwestern hospitality.

However, the QCCVB's primary activity is to positively impact the region's economy through convention, trade show and leisure travel expenditures and to provide quality services to visitors, the Quad-Cities' community, its residents and the bureau's membership.

Eager to Please

Formed in 1990, the QCCVB serves as the liaison to the multitude of event planners in the meeting, convention, sports and tourism industry in a two-state, six-city, three-county area. It also promotes tourism to its own residents, encouraging them to vacation in their own back yard, and it works diligently to keep reunions and local business meetings and conventions within its Quad-Cities' communities.

The QCCVB represents Scott County in Iowa and Rock Island and Mercer counties in Illinois. The six major cities represented are Davenport and Bettendorf in Iowa, and Moline, East Moline, Silvis and Rock Island in Illinois.

Top 10 Attractions

The top 10 reasons people choose the Quad-Cities for a vacation or weekend getaway include: the Mississippi River, festivals and special events, shopping, historical attractions, riverboat casinos, family activities, concerts, arts/culture/theater, John Deere attractions and outdoor recreation.

The Quad-Cities mostly attracts visitors from within a 300-mile radius, and they contribute an impressive $145 million dollars per year to the area's economy. The QCCVB also books more than 300 meetings and conventions each year. Here's what visitors have to say about the Quad-Cities experience.

"We had an agricultural dealer meeting that brought in about 6,000. They love coming to the Quad-Cities. It's affordable. I like to say it's the best kept secret here in the Midwest." – Paul Knedler, retired

guest relations manager, Deere & Company

"Everything ran perfectly. People enjoyed seeing the bald eagles and everyone was friendly and helpful. We look forward to our next trip to the Quad-Cities." – Gay Kuester, travel program manager, Brookfield Zoo, Chicago

"We are extremely happy with the Quad-Cities' area and visit several times a year. We have enjoyed all four seasons." – Mary Waytenick, Madison, Wis.

"Exceptional area, good restaurants, interesting sites to visit. The Bix Beiderbecke Memorial Jazz Festival is fantastic!" – John Peterson, Des Moines, Iowa

"We received a lot of comments nationally from attendees that were impressed with the Quad-Cities. Without the help of the Quad Cities CVB, we would not have had such a successful event." – Christina Daho, chairperson, Mississippi River Parkway Commission

The Mississippi River is one of the greatest assets of the Quad-Cities, and a favorite destination for tourists from around the region. The sparkling lights of the Centennial Bridge that links Davenport, Iowa, and Rock Island, Ill., above left, help create a stunning night scene. Below left, paddlewheelers of all shapes and sizes are a common sight in the region. Above, an aerial view of Davenport includes the Rock Island Arsenal Bridge, and Lock and Dam 15, the largest roller dam in the world.

QUAD CITIES AUTOMATIC SPRINKLER, INC. & MIDWEST COMPLIANCE CONSULTANTS, INC.

Above right, Quad Cities Automatic Sprinkler Design Manager Steve Farber uses CAD technology to custom design a building sprinkler system. Below right, Labor Manager Steve Daniels and Sprinkler Fitter Luke Linville perform maintenance on a sprinkler unit.

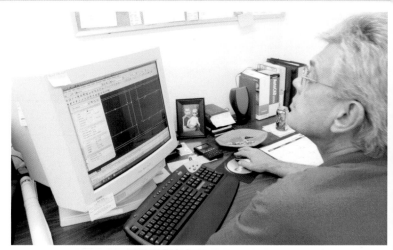

As owner of Quad Cities Automatic Sprinkler, Inc. (QCAS), and co-owner, with her husband, Scott, of Midwest Compliance Consultants, Inc. (MCCI), Jeffries is devoted to the business of saving lives. At the helm of the sprinkler business, she leads a team of veteran professionals who provide protection from fires capable of trapping and killing building occupants.

As president of the compliance company, she oversees accomplished consultants, including Scott, in providing professional guidance and management skills in the fields of construction and industry safety.

In Her Father's Footsteps

The name Van Gundy has been synonymous with fire sprinklers since 1958 when Julie's father Gordon — then a union pipefitter — established QCAS. Entrepreneurship was in Julie's blood. From childhood, she curiously observed her father conduct business, and as an adult, she worked side-by-side with him at QCAS and his other business ventures.

Upon his death in 2002, she made it her goal to carry on her father's original operation; to build it back to its glory days before his failing health prohibited further growth. Like her dad always did, and because the job of protecting lives is so important, Julie surrounds herself with the finest experts in the field. Her team of professional engineers, union sprinkler fitters,

and sales and office staff places emphasis on best safety equipment and practices for all projects large and small.

Personalized service by Jeffries and her team set QCAS apart from the competition. The company philosophy targets on-time or ahead-of-schedule delivery of all projects; and the advanced experience of the company's lead journeyman benefits clients through wise decisions that result in cost savings. Fire sprinkler requirements in today's building codes have led to tremendous growth in the industry and are aimed at keeping occupants safer from fire than ever before, especially in buildings where rapid

evacuation can be difficult.

As an active member of the National Fire Sprinkler Association (NFSA) and other industry groups, the company stays abreast of current fire protection issues and technological innovations to ensure they provide clients with the finest up-to-code systems. Upon Jeffries' insistence, continuous education for employees is necessary and mandatory.

Serving the entire Midwest, QCAS engineers customize each fire system through efficient, effective designs that meet all NFSA quality standards. Union-trained installers ensure flawless installations, proper maintenance and essential testing that keeps

every sprinkler fully functional and reliable. As a full service fire-sprinkler company, QCAS is capable of providing many system options, including wet, dry and foam, or combinations of systems, each offering its own distinct benefits and selected based on particular building needs and criteria.

Retrofits to existing systems are an equally important market to QCAS. By bringing systems up to code, building owners can realize discounts in insurance premiums, increased property value and superior safety protection.

Automatic fire sprinkler systems are widely recognized as the single most effective method for fighting the spread of fires in their early stages. Spaced throughout the ceilings of buildings, sprinklers actually are integrated networks of piping connected to a water supply. Unlike their predecessors, modern-day sprinklers are individually heat-activated, automatically operating only in areas where fire is located, and not throughout an entire building. They keep fires small, and prevent fast-developing fires capable of trapping and killing occupants.

According to the National Fire Protection Association, there never has been any multiple loss of life in a fully sprinklered building. Property losses are 85 percent less in residences with fire sprinklers compared to those without sprinklers. The combination of automatic sprinklers and early warnings systems in all buildings and residences could reduce overall injuries, loss of life and property damage by at least 50 percent.

Midwest Compliance Keeps Workers Safe

Midwest Compliance's lead Safety Consultant Scott Jeffries targets safety to protect companies' profits and workers' lives. If safety is doing its job, it's not easily seen — there are no injuries, missed workdays or lost

profits. Instead, companies experience lower insurance rates, fewer worker compensation claims and stabilized profits. As more and more companies are seeing safety as a good investment, MCCI rapidly is growing its list of clients who desire to meet and exceed environmental and occupational safety regulations.

Since 1992, the company has been customizing health, safety training and compliance needs for construction- and industrial-based businesses throughout the region. From the Environmental Protection Agency to the Occupational Health and Safety Administration (OSHA), laws drive safety, and MCCI works closely with companies and their employees to assure they understand and benefit from implementation of total safe practices.

MCCI serves clients part time and full time through myriad safety-related services. Highly educat-

ed consultants conduct OSHA compliance reviews, job hazard assessments, safety audits, Material Safety Data Sheets updates and on-site safety inspections. Specialty training services include development of complete safety, lock-out/tag-out and regulatory compliance programs, OSHA training, and educational programs for all at-risk occupations and equipment use. In addition, MCCI's diverse team is extremely adept in creating employee safety handbooks, conducting safety talks, leading safety meetings and developing emergency safety plans.

Together MCCI and QCAS complement each other, in that safety inspections are essential components of fire sprinkler system compliance regulations. It pays to be safe, and QCAS and MCCI are positioned to ensure that message is never forgotten.

Top left, keeping your buildings safe is the team from Quad Cities Automatic Sprinkler, from left, Brett Jeffries, Steve Farber, Steve Daniels, Luke Linville, Ray Cross, President Julie Van Gundy Jeffries, Mike Collins and Nicky Daniels. Left, keeping you safe on the job is the team from Midwest Compliance Consultants, from left, Tammy Collins, Beth Russell, Lead Safety Consultant Scott Jeffries, President Julie Van Gundy Jeffries and Nicky Daniels. Not pictured, Safety Consultant Randy Jespersen.

QUAD CITIES AUTOMATIC SPRINKLER, INC.

2 Kohles Court
Bettendorf, Iowa 52722
(563) 359-0341
www.qcasprinkler.com

MIDWEST COMPLIANCE CONSULTANTS, INC.

2 Kohles Court
Bettendorf, Iowa 52722
(563) 355-5489
www.mcci-safety.com

O UT OF THE DARKNESS COMES A LIGHT. THE MISSISSIPPI RIVER BEND REGION HAS COME A LONG WAY SINCE THE UNPRECEDENTED DOWNTURN OF THE AGRICULTURAL MANUFACTURING INDUSTRY IN THE EARLY 1980S. THE ECONOMIC OUTLOOK FOR WHAT WAS THEN "THE FARM IMPLEMENT CAPITAL OF

Above, the Quad City Development Group actively pursues smart growth throughout the eastern Iowa and western Illinois region, including Rock Island, forefront; and at the mammoth Rock Island Arsenal, seen directly across the river. Below, the group is involved in continual studies of regional bridges that are so important to future transportation needs of the region that is joined by the Mississippi River.

the world" was bleak. Plants closed, 22,000 jobs were lost, property values dropped, population fell and schools and local governments struggled with declining tax revenues.

The light arrived in the early 1990s as the governments and businesses of the Quad-Cities banded together to rejuvenate the area through aggressive marketing by the Quad City Development Group. Known as the "Best of Illinois and Iowa," the Quad-Cities is at the crossroads of the Midwest.

The U.S. Census Bureau ranks the area in the top 10 of Midwestern metropolitan areas to make a dramatic rebound from the 1980s. A factor in this turnaround has been the diversification of industry. A wide variety of manufacturers and service industries have been attracted to the area in the last 10 years because of its great location, the low cost of doing business and the strong work ethic of the population.

Non-farm business entering the Quad-Cities increased 5.9 percent from 1990 to 1995.

Today, the light shines brightly. The job base is growing. Population is gaining. Retail is soaring. Property values are rising. Even unemployment is at a record low. The Quad City Development Group has been a driving force in this success. By approaching economic development as a region, the development group has suc-

ceeded in bringing 15,000 jobs and more than $1 billion in new investments into the area over the last 10 years.

Selling Our Values

T he development group is armed with great selling points appealing highly to new and expanding businesses considering relocation or growth in the region, which includes Scott county in eastern Iowa, and Rock

Island, Henry and Mercer counties in western Illinois.

Among the region's strong points is a high-quality, stable and productive labor force. In fact, workforce productivity here is 37 percent higher than the national average. More than 84 percent of the labor force has a high school education, and 38 percent hold four-year or higher college degrees.

Blessed with a highly favorable cost of living, the region consistently ranks below the national average in all major cost categories, which translates into many practical advantages.

Recently, the Quad-Cities' housing cost ranked 9.8 percent below the national average. The overall cost of living is 13.4 percent below the national average.

The list of benefits goes on and on. Development space is growing. Industrial parks are in place.

Plus, outstanding health and academic institutions and a wide range of cultural, sporting and recreational opportunities create a well-rounded climate for both businesses and families.

Working for You

Armed with these and many other statistics that showcase the assets of the region, the Quad City Development Group sets priorities by consensus among local colleagues in economic development, and then goes for the gold. The objectives are three-fold:

• To make sure people have good quality jobs by marketing the area externally to attract new investments and jobs to the area

• To ensure companies have a favorable business climate so they can expand and grow

• To counsel local communities on becoming more attractive to

existing and potential employers.

It's not just business that benefits from the group's efforts. Everyone wins in this cycle of success. For instance, every new or retained job in the Quad-Cities provides jobs for residents. Those new payroll dollars buy goods, services, homes, cars and much more from area businesses, which improves the overall economic prosperity of the area. With that, property values rise, ensuring a more stable financial future for residents and businesses. With more business comes a broader sharing of tax burdens.

Those dollars help our schools, local government and culture prosper, providing improved quality of life. In turn, our region attracts more qualified workers to the area to fill jobs.

A Regional Endeavor

The Quad City Development Group is a nonprofit organization supported by local governments and the private sector. For more than 40 years, it has been the only organization that markets the region as one community to businesses all over North America and Europe. The group works closely with various chambers of commerce and community economic development staffs and remains the eco-

nomic development umbrella for the Quad-Cities.

To target industries most likely to find the area attractive, the development group used a cluster study to select targeted industries and developed a highly focused marketing plan to attract these businesses. The plan incorporates a comprehensive Web site, advertising in specialized publications of interest to targeted firms, direct mail, telemarketing and, most significantly, person-to-person visits to qualified prospects. The group also participates in trade shows, trips and other marketing efforts in cooperation with the Illinois and Iowa state economic development agencies.

The group's other efforts include annual trips to Washington, D.C., to help promote regional needs among federal legislators and agencies. It also works to increase the workload and preserve jobs at the Rock Island Arsenal, the second largest employer in the Quad-Cities, and one of two such military arsenals and manufacturing facilities in the entire country.

The region is indeed at the crossroads of the Midwest – within a day's drive are nearly 40 million consumers. Perfect for businesses and families, it is truly the best of Illinois and Iowa.

Cultural opportunities, such as the state-of-the-art entertainment complex The MARK of the Quad Cities in Moline, help attract companies and their employees. Below, the Quad City Development Group was involved in securing Swiss Valley Farms headquarters as the first tenant in the Iowa Research Industrial Park in Davenport.

QUAD CITY DEVELOPMENT GROUP

1830 Second Avenue
Suite 200
Rock Island, Illinois 61201
(563) 326-1005 (Iowa)
(309) 788-7436 (Illinois)
www.quadcities.org

DAVENPORT MUSEUM OF ART AND

THE FIGGE

1737 West 12th Street
Davenport, Iowa 52804
(563) 326-7804
www.art-dma.org

FAMILY MUSEUM OF ARTS AND SCIENCE

2900 Learning Campus Drive
Bettendorf, Iowa 52722
(563) 344-4106
www.familymuseum.org

PUTNAM MUSEUM/ IMAX® THEATRE

1717 West 12th Street
Davenport, Iowa 52804
(563) 324-1054
www.putnam.org

Top right, the Davenport Museum of Art's more than 3,500 works of art present a multitude of opportunities for cultural growth. Below, kids make a cloud at the Family Museum of Arts and Science, just one of this museum's many interactive educational offerings. Below right, the high-tech IMAX® Theatre enhances the learning experiences presented at the Putnam Museum.

history, artifacts and collections, or in being wowed by the wonders of science and technology, you can find it here.

New Life for the Arts

C reated in 1925, the Davenport Municipal Art Gallery was the first municipal art gallery in Iowa. A gift of 334 paintings to the City of Davenport, Iowa, from Charles August Ficke formed the basis of the permanent collection.

Today, the collections of the Davenport Museum of Art have grown more than 10-fold to include more than 3,500 works of art from many cultures and periods of history. The museum is now poised for its next phase of growth – its relocation to the heart of downtown Davenport and transformation into The Figge art museum, named in recognition of a $12 million gift from the V.O. and Elizabeth Kahl Figge Foundation.

Designated to open in the summer of 2005, the center is a stunning, new 100,000-square-foot facility along the banks of the Mississippi River. The move and expansion enables the museum to ensure proper care of its collection well into the 22nd century. Moreover, the new facility is destined to become a regional landmark building where people of all ages can gather to create, view and experience art.

Created for Kids

F rom the moment you walk into the colorful, lively environment of the Family Museum of Arts and Science, you know you're going to have fun. Bettendorf residents, who passed a city bond referendum in 1994, as well as private donors, validated their commitment to lifelong learning to make

the museum a reality. Thanks to that effort, children from throughout the region develop lifelong learning skills. More than 115,000 annually visit the facility that cleverly melds arts and science together into integral, illustrative stories.

Geared for children 12 and younger, families and caregivers, the variety of activities includes five permanent exhibits. *Busy Bodies: Healthy Choices* puts some fun into learning about good health. *Homestead* has kids howling as they touch a 10 foot tornado and learn other fascinating agricultural and weather facts. *Rhythm Alley* rocks with sound. *The Garden* stimulates the senses of youngsters younger than five. *Kingdom for Kids* is the museum's ultra-modern outdoor playground. In addition, interactive rotating exhibits; a performing-arts program in dance for children and adults; in-school presentations; and on-site classes keep the ever-changing museum a great place for return visits.

From History to High Tech

T he Putnam Museum and IMAX® Theatre has been providing the region with quality-of-life experiences since 1867. It is the primary repository for the area's unique treasures, with more than 160,000 artifacts and specimens that tell the stories of the region, the people who live here and their

connections to the world.

The latest addition to the Museum is the colossal IMAX® Theatre, featuring 270 sloped, stadium-style seats; a screen six stories high and seven stories wide; a six-speaker, 10,000 watt digital sound system; and the Academy Award®-winning IMAX projection system.

The Museum's permanent exhibits, *Black Earth/Big River, Hall of Mammals, River, Prairie and People,* and *Asian/Egyptian Gallery,* immerse you in a wealth of culture and natural history.

There's something for everyone at the Putnam: Heritage Theatre® brings the gallery experience to life with weekly performances, and the Education Department provides school services to 19 counties.

With more than 275,000 visitors annually, the Putnam Museum and IMAX® Theatre provides a unique multi-sensory experience it calls "Entertainment for your mind."

Oregionality

I'T'S A PLACE FULL OF FRIENDLY FACES AND STUNNING DESIGN FEATURES. THE ATMOSPHERE IS ULTRA-CLEAN AND AIRY. VISITORS BROWSE REGIONAL ART AND CHAT WITH VOLUNTEERS WHO ENTHUSIASTI-CALLY PROMOTE THE ASSETS OF THE REGION. THE RESTAURANT BUSTLES WITH CHEERFUL ACTIVITY.

QUAD CITY INTERNATIONAL AIRPORT & METROPOLITAN AIRPORT AUTHORITY OF ROCK ISLAND COUNTY

**P.O. Box 9009
Moline, Illinois 61265
(309) 764-9621
www.qcairport.com**

Even the advertising is fresh and reflective of regional economic vitality. Only in the Quad-Cities could an airport become an extension of the famous Midwestern hospitality that often astonishes visitors from around the globe. This is the Quad City International Airport, owned and operated by the Metropolitan Airport Authority of Rock Island County, and it is a point of pride for all in the region.

From Gypsy to Giant

It was 1919 when the landing wheels of flying machines first touched down on a field that would become the Quad City International Airport. "Gypsy fliers" created a good business selling air rides to curious residents.

No one could have known that from this 200-acre Rock River Valley pasture, a full-service, 2,600-acre international airport would blossom.

In 1926, Moline seized the opportunity to win a place on the air map as a pickup facility for the U.S. Postal Service's new airmail delivery. Among its first famous visitors was U.S. Air Mail Pilot Charles Lindbergh, who received a hero's welcome when his Spirit of St. Louis plane touched down in 1927, just months after his famous solo flight across the Atlantic Ocean. Once on the map, the airport continued to flourish.

Easy To Get There

Today, the Quad City International Airport ranks 140th out of 600 commercial airports in the country, based on passengers served. Between 1990 and 2003, the annual passenger count grew from 300,000 to

almost 400,000.

Airport officials credit its low-fare carriers for changing the whole dynamic of how people travel. The airport is fortunate to host these low-cost carriers, which have contributed to a steady increase of passengers.

Customers in dozens of counties throughout eastern Iowa and western Illinois choose the Quad City International Airport as their departure point, crediting its convenience, accessibility and affordability.

Nationally recognized carriers have been mainstays over the years. You can get just about anywhere from here by making a single connection at one of seven larger hubs.

In addition, freight operations and general aviation for private and charter flights are centrally located on the property. The airport's international status translates into convenience

through on-site customs services, a feature of particular importance to local corporations that fly globally on private and chartered jets.

A Regional Showpiece

The airport authority debuted a new $17 million expansion in 2000 and continues to add new routes and services that benefit travelers.

Amenities include a partnership with Quad-City Arts for a revolving exhibit of local and regional artists, a contemporary gift shop, a full-service restaurant and a business center for working travelers. Airport authority personnel work diligently to present their jewel as a gateway to the community. After all, when business and leisure travelers come to the Quad-Cities, the airport is the first and last place they experience.

Today's top-class facility is leaving them extremely impressed.

Above, visitors find solace in viewing the revolving art exhibit that showcases the talents of local and regional artists. Above left, the airport's attractive, open-air terminal. Below, today's Quad City International Airport is the airport of choice for business and leisure travelers from eastern Iowa and western Illinois.

THE AWARD-WINNING *QUAD-CITY TIMES* IS THE LIFE-BLOOD OF THE EASTERN IOWA/WESTERN ILLINOIS METROPOLITAN COMMUNITIES OF DAVENPORT AND BETTENDORF IN IOWA AND ROCK ISLAND, MOLINE AND EAST MOLINE IN ILLINOIS. READERS AND BUSINESSES LOOK TO THE *QUAD-CITY TIMES*

for its balanced coverage of local and national news and advertising.

The *Quad-City Times* traces its history to the birth of the *Davenport Democrat* in 1855 and the *Blue Ribbon News* in 1878. The *Blue Ribbon News*, which was by then known as the *Davenport Daily Times*, became part of Lee Enterprises in 1899, when it was purchased by A.W. Lee. The purchase price was $20,000. Lee's approach to newspaper publishing included a willingness to experiment with all aspects of the paper, not just the editorial functions.

As a result of A.W. Lee's foresight, the company acquired a rich editorial and management legacy that exists to this day.

Among the most significant philosophies were integrity in news reporting, the encouragement of risk-taking in pioneering new ventures of procedures, motivating employees to improve their skills and performance, encouraging more interesting advertising, and a tradition of service to the public and community.

E.P. Adler was a protege of Lee and became editor, then publisher in 1901 of the *Davenport Times*. Eventually, he would become president of the Lee Syndicate in 1907. His son, Philip D. Adler, would become president of Lee Enterprises in 1960 and retire as publisher of the *Times-Democrat* in 1969.

In the early 1900s, the *Daily Times* had tough competition in Davenport, a town with five newspapers and many German language or specialty publications at the turn of the century. Mergers also were becoming a sign of the times, and in 1915 Lee purchased the *Davenport Democrat and Leader* to join the *Daily Times* among Lee Syndicate newspapers.

Above, the *Quad-City Times* moved to 500 East Third Street, in Davenport, in 1990. Below, more than 163,000 readers start their Sunday with the region's largest newspaper.

On October 2, 1951, the Times and Democrat publishing companies merged into Davenport Newspapers, Inc. The paper went into the morning field and was renamed the *Morning Democrat*. The *Times* continued as an afternoon edition.

On June 1, 1964, the *Democrat* and the *Times* were merged into one paper, the *Times-Democrat*, publishing two editions, one in the morning and another in the afternoon. In the early 1970s, support for a single name for the entire region was growing. Coupled with the emerging importance of Bettendorf as the fourth "quad" city and a desire to drop any assumed political affiliation, the newspaper's leadership renamed the *Times-Democrat* as the *Quad-City Times* in 1974.

One newspaper — many roles

The *Quad-City Times* includes several key departments that make up the day-to-day business of running a quality newspaper. The editorial and advertising departments work in tandem – together they create a fluid, vital newspaper.

Editorial includes several subdepartments that perform a myriad of tasks: Local news is covered by *Times* reporters, freelance writers and photographers; the features department produces rich and informative sections throughout the year on such varied topics as health, home and garden and entertainment; national and local sporting events are covered by the sports department; the editorial page provides a forum for community mem-

O r e g i o n a l i t y

bers to voice their opinions on topical issues.

Similarly, the *Times* advertising department also includes several smaller groups that form the nucleus of the department – retail, classified, online and marketing. Businesses and individuals alike use advertisements and classified ads to promote their messages. With the proliferation of the Internet, the *Times* stayed ahead of the curve, introducing QCTimes.com in 1998. In addition to first-rate editorial and news copy, the *Times* also produces a wide array of sections and niche publications tailored to readers and advertisers.

'Big Blue'

Today, page designers, editors and artists send computer-designed pages and ads directly to the plate room where negatives are output and used to create printing plates that go on the press.

Affectionately known as "Big Blue," the Goss Colorliner is a computerized offset press that uses state-of-the-art technology to run up to 75,000 papers an hour. Weighing 1.9 million pounds, the huge press is 96 feet long by 43 feet high. Paper winding through the press can reach speeds up to 26 miles per hour.

Our market today and how we cover it

The Quad-City market of 350,000 people is perhaps the most unusual collection of river communities in the United States. Joined by one of the nation's most celebrated rivers, the Quad-Cities is known as the place "where the Mississippi River flows east to west." In fact, the river flows westward between Illinois and Iowa and almost equally separates the population on both sides.

Five cities – Davenport and Bettendorf in Iowa and Rock Island, Moline and East Moline in Illinois

– make up the core of the Quad-Cities and readership of the *Quad-City Times*. To the north, the city of Clinton, Iowa, Clinton County and several neighboring Illinois communities make up the newspaper's "Gateway" edition coverage area. To the south, the newspaper circulates into Muscatine, Iowa. The complexities associated with covering two states, several communities of similar size, corporate headquarters, minor league sports and several rural and urban counties keeps the *Times* newsroom hustling.

Interesting facts

- In 1973, the *Times* became the first newspaper in the world to be produced by computer.
- Bill Wundram, who writes seven columns a week, has worked at the *Times* for 59 years.
- The newspaper is the title sponsor

of one of America's great road races. The *Quad-City Times Bix 7*, a seven-mile race through Davenport, attracts more than 20,000 runners each July from all over the world.

- Davenport's city-owned baseball stadium was named in 1971 after the newspaper's legendary sports editor John O'Donnell, who became known for his "Dear Joe" columns during world war II.
- The Quad-City Times Strategic Business Unit (SBU) also publishes: *Bettendorf News; Quad-City Business Journal; On the River; Wheels for You; Thrifty Nickel; Work for You; Muscatine Journal; Classic Images; Films of the Golden Age and The Post*
- The *Quad-City Times* was recently named "Newspaper of the Year" for the second consecutive year by Suburban Newspapers of America.

Above, the *Quad-City Times* sponsors the Bix 7, one of the top 10 road races in the country. Below, the *Quad-City Times* prints on "Big Blue," a state-of-the-art press that can run up to 75,000 papers per hour.

Quad-City Times

QUAD-CITY TIMES

500 East Third Street Davenport, Iowa 52801 (563) 383-2200 www.qctimes.com

make her job oh-so fine. Contributing to the quality of life in the Quad-Cities' community since 1989, the RDA, a nonprofit corporation affiliated with Davenport's Rhythm City Casino, has distributed more than $30 million to more than 400 organizations through its Grant Awards Program.

By Iowa law, only a nonprofit organization can hold a gambling license, and operating casinos must share gaming revenue with that nonprofit, which, in turn, distributes it to community causes.

Extending Its Reach

Because of this unique partnership, front-line community services; the arts, culture and education; and economic development have flourished throughout the Quad-Cities and Scott County.

For example, there is hardly a downtown Davenport River Renaissance project that RDA contributions have not touched. The building of the new Figge Art Museum, two parking structures, riverfront skywalk and the renovation of historic John O'Donnell Stadium are but a few projects that have greatly benefited from RDA dollars.

When it comes to technology, the RDA brought the nonprofit community into the 21st century. In the schools, the RDA was a pioneer at funding technology. With grants provided to the Mississippi Bend Area Education Agency, RDA helped make Scott the first county in the state to have all schools internet accessible.

RDA has granted millions to special needs, daycare and preschool programs, historic preservation, parks and recreation, health

Recent recipients of Riverboat Development Authority grants include, clockwise from top: Hand-in-Hand, for Tessa's Place, a daycare facility for special-needs children; The Figge art museum, for its 70,000-square-foot facility under construction in the heart of downtown Davenport and Schuetzen Park Gilde, for preservation of a native timber forest at the Schuetzen Park Historic Site.

care, the arts, public safety, neighborhood development, libraries and museums, and so much more.

Throughout Scott County communities, contributions of RDA dollars are helping make impressive and exciting improvements. Illinois benefits, too. If a project serves residents of Scott County but is based in the Illinois Quad-Cities, it is eligible for consideration.

A sampling of riverboat dollars at work in communities shows the diversity of causes the grants have supported as of September 2003: Davenport: Streetscape and flower baskets; Center For Active Seniors

pavilion; Mississippi Valley Blues Festival; John Bloom sculpture on the Davenport riverfront bike path; Hilltop Park; Quad Cities Sports Center; Village of East Davenport historical lighting; LeClaire House restoration; Quad City Arts Festival of Trees; and DREAM Program home-ownership assistance.
Bettendorf: Community Center gazebo; Bettendorf Library; Family Museum of Arts and Science; Splash Landing; Armstrong School Year-Round Program; and "Bring It On Home" Campaign.
Illinois Quad-Cities: Urban

Indian Tribal Organization; Quad City Helicopter Emergency Medical Service; Quad City Botanical Center; American Red Cross-Quad City Chapter; Riverview Food Bank; and Col. Davenport Home Restoration.

Scott County: Safety education for children; Senior Light Tour; Walnut Grove Pioneer Village; Walnut Grove Heritage Days; the Wapsi Environmental Center; Duck Creek Watershed Project; Bi-Centennial Trail markers; and enhanced 911.

Blue Grass: Blue Grass Community Club hall improvements; park pavilion and playground; and welcome signs.

Buffalo: Senior housing complex; riverfront improvements; public safety equipment; and historical museum.

Dixon: American Legion Hall; Christmas lights; and playground equipment.

Donahue: American Legion Hall; ball diamond; and public safety equipment.

Durant: Fire truck; Feldhahn Park; and Fitness Trail.

Eldridge: Headquarters building of the Scott County Library System; public art projects; North Scott High School Veterans' Memorial; Centennial Park Playground and Shelter.

LeClaire: Iowa Welcome Center at LeClaire; Lone Star Steamboat; riverfront improvements; Water Tower Park; Civic Center; and Buffalo Bill Museum.

Long Grove: Long Grove Heritage Park; community center; public art project; and playground equipment.

Maysville: Community Center; warning siren; and Maysville Park.

McCausland: Baseball diamond; park concession stand; police computer; and recycling bins.

New Liberty: Fire station; Christmas lights; and Liberty Park.

Parkview: Public art project and recreational fields.

Princeton: Riverfront enhancement and Boll's General Store restoration into community center.

Riverdale: Riverdale Bicentennial Park and fire department cascade tanks.

Walcott: Tennis courts at Wescott Park; Walcott Forever Green; Walcott American Legion building; and Victory Park playground.

Diverse Causes, Diverse Board

Along with Chamberlin, 14 volunteers from all parts of Scott County serve on the RDA board of directors. Its makeup remains highly reflective of the community's personality. The RDA operates somewhat like a community foundation, with the exception that it has a single source of income – the Rhythm City Casino.

With a firm belief in the power of grassroots efforts, RDA provides the money, and residents drive the manpower to get the job done. Like yeast is to bread, a grant provides a solid foundation for turning a dream into reality.

Got A Dream?

Twice each year the RDA accepts grant proposals from nonprofit agencies, educational institutions and governmental departments for programs benefiting residents of Scott County. By design, the grant application process is easy. As Chamberlin puts it, the RDA funds good projects, not well-written applications. It reviews every group's vision, and, by consensus, decides which requests will most improve quality of life in the Quad-Cities.

The board also spends time bringing people into collaborative efforts that prioritize community needs. It educates and focuses groups to work together on projects that can provide a greater impact than a single request.

In the great debate of gambling, Chamberlin says it was the state's wise initiative to give back casino profits to community causes that has delivered benefits that far outweigh any negatives. She calls it "better living through riverboat giving," and since 1989, its value has, indeed, become clear.

RDA dollars go to all types of projects, including these street scapes in downtown Davenport, above, and the weekly Senior Meal Program at Bethel AME Church on 11th Street in Davenport.

RIVERBOAT DEVELOPMENT AUTHORITY
Blackhawk Hotel
200 East Third Street
Davenport, Iowa 52801
(563) 328-8078
www.riverboatauthority.com

RiverCenter

Adler Theatre

**136 East Third Street
Davenport, Iowa 52801
(563) 326-8500
www.adlertheatre.com**

Davenport's 2,400-seat historic Adler Theatre, below, plays host to scores of celebrity headliners, including this sold-out B.B. King performance, above right. Below right, the RiverCenter is a multiple-use facility that supports Davenport's mission of growth, development and enhanced quality of life for the Quad-City community.

The theatre was refurbished to its art-deco glory in 1986 and became part of a dominant convention and entertainment complex owned by the City of Davenport, Iowa. Original crystal chandeliers, a gold-leaf ceiling, and black ebony, walnut and marble detailing are meticulously restored. In contrast, state-of-the-art acoustics create a near perfect theatrical environment.

The renaming of the theatre celebrated a major contribution to the cause by Lee Enterprises, publisher of the *Quad-City Times* newspaper, and honored E.P. and Philip Adler, who served as publishers for 48 years. The theatre's rebirth was hailed as magnificent, a true masterpiece and since has hosted celebrity headliners,

Dick Oberg Photography

Broadway greats, comedians, dance and symphony performances. However, its completion was only the beginning.

Blending Old and New

The conception of its neighbor and partner, the RiverCenter, happened nearly simultaneously with the donation of the theatre by the city to the RiverCenter for the Performing Arts. The mission of this nonprofit group was to raise money to restore the theatre and build a venue that would attract trade shows, meetings and special events to the heart of downtown.

Combining the two notions completed the dream. The original RiverCenter opened in 1983. Designed with a light and airy industrial feel, it is a unique structure featuring a 13,200-square-foot, column-free exhibit hall, six meeting rooms, a commercial-use kitchen and an atrium/reception area.

In 1994, the RiverCenter expanded by 79,000 square feet to include

an additional 32,400-square-foot, column-free exhibit hall with a 9,000 square-foot-concourse/reception area, four breakout meeting rooms and an executive board room.

The Heart of Davenport

The expansion presents a stunning view of the Mississippi River and is a favorite place for bald eagle watching during the winter months. A system of enclosed skywalks connects the climate-controlled convention facility to a parking ramp, two hotels and, of course, the Adler Theatre.

By blending the proud tradition of the elegant, sophisticated atmosphere of the Adler with the modern flexibility of the beautiful RiverCenter, this multiple-use facility supports the city's mission of growth and development, while enhancing the quality of life for residents and visitors alike.

W ITH A HISTORY DATING BACK TO 1884, RIVERMONT COLLEGIATE IS AN INTELLECTUAL AND CULTURAL LANDMARK IN THE QUAD-CITIES. LOCATED ON THE FORMER JOSEPH BETTENDORF ESTATE ON SUNSET DRIVE IN BETTENDORF, RIVERMONT COLLEGIATE IS A COEDUCATIONAL,

**1821 Sunset Drive
Bettendorf, Iowa 52722
(563) 359-1366
www.rivermontcollegiate.com**

nonsectarian, independent college preparatory school for preschool through 12th grade students. This unique school offers a nurturing, caring, and safe environment where students develop intellect, character, and creativity. Long recognized for its vision in providing a broad range of intellectual, physical, artistic, and cultural challenges, Rivermont Collegiate enjoys an excellent reputation for preparing students for leadership in a variety of arenas, depending on their interests.

Left, Rivermont Collegiate's beautiful campus. Below, bottom, a Middle School class meets in the historic Wallace House. Below, the atrium of Becherer Hall, the new Lower School and Performing Arts Center.

Built on Tradition

T he stately Joseph Bettendorf mansion houses the High School and administrative offices. The school's newest facility, Becherer Hall, a state-of-the-art Lower School building and Performing Arts Center, which is also home to a resident theater group, opened in 2001. A graphic and performing arts instruction center, located in the classic former Carriage House, Wallace House, the site of most Middle School classes, and a well-equipped gymnasium, which is used widely by the community, complete the 9 acre campus.

In partnership with students, parents and faculty, Rivermont Collegiate encourages students to aspire to excellence, assists each student in the realization of his or her fullest potential, and guides each student in the development of a wholesome self-concept and a dedication to lifelong learning. By preparing students for colleges and universities well suited to their individual needs, interests, and aspirations, Rivermont Collegiate helps to ensure students' success.

Rivermont Collegiate views the family as the primary source of tra-

ditions, celebrations, and values for its children. The role of the school is to affirm that each individual has a valuable and distinct identity and to help students appreciate their own strengths and those of others. Rivermont Collegiate helps students of diverse backgrounds attain a level of intellectual proficiency and cultural awareness that compares favorably with accomplishments at the most competitive college preparatory schools in the nation.

Preparing Students for Tomorrow

T o prepare students for the challenges of college and adult life, Rivermont offers a complete range of college counseling experiences designed to help the young adolescent focus on college preparation as a goal, gather data, analyze personal curricular choices, and meet deadlines essential to acceptance in the college of his or her choice. With record high composite ACT and SAT scores year after year, Rivermont graduates boast 100 percent admission to competitive four-year colleges annually.

Rivermont Collegiate offers four distinct but complementary levels of education: Early Childhood (preschool), Lower School (kindergarten-grade 5), Middle School (grades 6-8), and High School (grades 9-12). Enrollment for the

2003-2004 school year is expected to reach 260 students. Rivermont's commitment to maintaining limited class size provides students much individualized instruction and attention. Although primarily known for its outstanding academic curriculum, Rivermont's athletic program continues to grow, offering youth programs in soccer, basketball, volleyball, track, golf, and other lifestyle sports. Rivermont is a member of the Iowa High School Athletic Association.

While Rivermont Collegiate is proud of its extraordinary campus and the architectural and historic treasures it holds, over its long history, it has been its students and faculty that have been its greatest pride. The social and cultural diversity represented in its student body is unique in the Quad-Cities. Admission to Rivermont Collegiate long has been academically competitive. While much personal and academic support is available to its students, much is expected of them. Many excel in art, drama, music, and athletics and have gone on to pursue notable careers in the humanities, arts and sciences, business, medicine, and law. Rivermont even produced the first female Minor League umpire.

As the nation's largest women-led fraternal benefit society, Royal Neighbors of America (RNA) became a strong force long before women could vote. Its mission, making financial security and independence a reality for women, was unheard of at the time.

**230 16th Street
Rock Island, Illinois 61201
(309) 788-4561
www.royalneighbors.org**

RNA camps and chapters take part in the Society's Teddy Bear Program, top right, which, to date, has donated more than 3,000 teddy bears to hospitals, shelters and police and fire departments for children in stressful situations. Above, JOIN HANDS DAY, an annual day of volunteerism sponsored by America's fraternal benefit societies and the Points of Light Foundation, bridges generation gaps with projects that help neighborhoods. Bottom right, the bronze doors of the RNA National Headquarters serve as a warm welcome to staff and visitors. The carved figures on the door portray neighborliness, protection and sympathy.

Founded in 1888 as a social organization for the wives of a men-only fraternal benefit society, the idea of forming a like organization for women became the group's focus in 1895.

The Society was formed "to bring joy and comfort into many homes that might otherwise today be dark and cheerless ... by affording the mother an opportunity to provide protection upon her life."

Neighbors helping neighbors became the mantra of the progressive women, and today, RNA remains the country's largest fraternal benefit society dedicated to serving the needs of women and those they care about.

Financial Protection Plus More

With more than 200,000 members in 41 states and the District of Columbia, the society, a nonprofit membership organization, provides financial products, member benefits and social and volunteer programs that serve communities.

RNA's portfolio offers life insurance, annuities and IRAs to women, men and children. Its subsidiary company, American Fraternal Financial Services, Inc., expands the line to include long-term care, disability and medical supplemental insurance, mutual funds and other specialty products.

What differentiates the Society from other financial entities is its outreach programs, sponsorships and advocacy. Community involvement has been a cornerstone of RNA from its start. Throughout its existence, RNA has had a unique opportunity to influence women's rights. For example, RNA's scholarship pro-

grams contributed more than $1.7 million to make the dream of higher education a reality for its members.

RNA sponsors such initiatives as Habitat for Humanity and its Women Building A Legacy Program. In addition, localized camps and chapters around the nation contribute to their communities through such activities as the Society's Matching Funds Program, which helps raise funds for worthy causes.

RNA's history is enhanced through its belief in preserving, protecting and growing the financial assets and well-being of its members. Volunteer opportunities and community enrichment continue to provide meaningful outlets for today's women.

RNA's Six Guiding Principles

RNA's emblem, unchanged for more than 100 years, is

a symbol that represents the values most important to the pioneering women who founded the Society. The generations of women following their example have held fast to the vision. The blue petal, cross and lily of the valley represent "faith"; the yellow petal and handshake mean "unselfishness"; the green petal and sword represent "courage"; the purple petal and crown stand for "endurance"; the white petal and shield symbolize "modesty"; and the center with its cross represents "morality."

FAMILY AND HOME - THEY'RE TWO OF OUR MOST VALUED ASSETS, AND WHAT RUHL&RUHL REALTORS IS ALL ABOUT. SINCE 1862, THE RUHL FAMILY HAS BEEN HELPING FAMILIES IN THE QUAD-CITIES REGION.

RUHL&RUHL

REALTORS
5403 Victoria Avenue
Davenport, Iowa 52807
(563) 441-5200
www.ruhl-ruhl.com

Above, President Caroline Ruhl of Ruhl&Ruhl REALTORS is the fourth generation of Ruhls to lead the family business.

At left, in this 1898 photo, John Ruhl, on the right, began what would become a Quad-Cities entrepreneurial family legacy as co-owner of the Schaefer & Ruhl grocery store in Davenport.

Below, Ruhl&Ruhl REALTORS Matt Schwind and Teresa Harris are both Ruhl&Ruhl managers.

Innovators

Ruhl&Ruhl has been the first to use a number of technologies to make the home buying experience easier for its clients. The company was first to have all its listings on the Info Line at (563) 359-1999 or (800) 897-INFO. It was the first to market homes on the Internet and continuously offers more information and ease of use on its web site at www.ruhl-ruhl.com. It was the first and still is the only company in the region offering written service guarantees.

Ruhl&Ruhl Values

The company's seven core values – integrity; caring and challenging; commitment to client satisfaction; embracing change and continuous learning; loyalty; extraordinary quality; and community involvement – serve as the glue that holds the company together. These shared values provide all sales associates and staff a common bond and focus that will carry the company forward ... for at least **another** 141 years.

It all started in a little German grocery store in west Davenport from which insurance and real estate also were sold. Four generations and thousands of homes later, Caroline Ruhl leads Ruhl&Ruhl REALTORS today. She follows her father, Charles A. Ruhl, who succeeded his father, C. Arthur Ruhl, who also succeeded his father, John G. Ruhl. In addition, sister companies are led by family members: Ruhl & Ruhl Commercial Company, operated by Chuck Ruhl, Jr. and John Ruhl; and Ruhl & Ruhl Insurance, led by Mike Lischer and Scott Saveraid.

Ruhl&Ruhl REALTORS has grown to more than 260 sales associates, 50 employees and nine offices, yet their commitment to providing service with quality, value and integrity remains firmly rooted.

Real Estate Services

Ruhl&Ruhl annually sells more than 3,000 homes in eastern Iowa and western Illinois. The company has residential sales offices in Davenport, Bettendorf, Clinton, Muscatine, DeWitt, Maquoketa, and Iowa City, Iowa; and in Moline, Illinois. In addition to residential sales, the company offers services in relocation, new home sales, land development, farm sales, senior services, home services, and mortgage services.

"Our People are the Difference"

The people at Ruhl&Ruhl are committed to making the home buying and home selling experience easy, fun and hassle free. "Our clients need sales associates they can trust who will be their knowledgeable advocates, guiding them through the home sale or home purchase process. Our people really care about our clients and strive to exceed every expectation. At Ruhl&Ruhl, our people are the difference," says Caroline Ruhl.

RUSSELL CONSTRUCTION COMPANY

**1414 Mississippi Boulevard
Bettendorf, Iowa 52722
(563) 355-1845
www.russellco.com**

Top right, Russell Construction received the 2003 Master Builder of Iowa "Masters Award" for the $27 million expansion and renovation to Genesis Medical Center East Campus, Above right, the Russell executive team, from top left, Randy Clarahan, Steve Daxon, Jim Russell and Kathy Mirocha. Above, American Bank & Trust Co. selected Russell Construction to build its first Iowa branch in Davenport, Iowa.

By developing strong partnerships with clients, subcontractors and communities, Russell's team of experienced and motivated construction professionals have completed diverse projects in more than 20 states.

According to President Jim Russell, the company defines success as a result of the people and organizations it has partnered with over the years:

• The clients who put their faith in Russell's abilities to transform their vision into reality;

• The employees who reach higher and work harder on every project and relationship;

• The subcontractors who share their passion for excellence and customer satisfaction;

• The numerous civic and charitable organizations that provide rewarding opportunities for the company and its employees to build strong communities.

Growth by Design

R ussell looks at its customers as partners, closely listening to their needs and responding to their concerns.

It's an attitude shared by everyone at Russell – from the workers on the job site to support personnel in its offices.

And although Russell has received many awards, what it is really proud of is receiving the trust and respect of clients who continually seek out the company for construction and project management.

For example, in 1994, Russell completed its first building project for Genesis Health System. Since that time, the company has been involved in more than 155 Genesis projects.

People. Process. Pride.

A lot has changed in the construction process since 1983, but Russell's commitment to continually improving the process for all parties involved keeps them at the forefront of the industry.

With each completed project, something new is learned: A new way to improve construction efficiencies; a smarter way to integrate technology into the process; a better way to communicate with clients and people in the field.

Russell embraces a "best-in-class" philosophy about hiring, training and motivating its people to make a difference.

You can see it in their creativity and attention to detail. You sense it in their satisfaction of a job well done. You can feel it in the pride they take in each project, every relationship and the communities in which they live and work.

And as Russell looks to the future, it continues to define suc-

cess in terms of the three things it values most – people, process and pride.

Russell Construction Company is a Midwest leader in design, construction and management services for premier clients throughout the region.

A sampling of their clients and projects include Genesis Medical Center, Deere & Company, St. Ambrose University, Figge Arts Center, Mississippi Valley Regional Blood Center, John O'Donnell Stadium, Von Maur and numerous Walgreens stores throughout the Midwest. Today Russell is celebrating 20 years of building people, process and pride throughout our community.

"A ROCK PILE CEASES TO BE A ROCK PILE WHEN SOMEONE CONTEMPLATES IT WITH A CATHEDRAL IN MIND." THIS PROFOUND THOUGHT MAY HAVE COME FROM THE MIND OF A FRENCH PHILOSOPHER, BUT IT IS THE VERY FOUNDATION BY WHICH THE SEDONA GROUP BUILDS THE POTENTIAL OF EACH PERSON

THE SEDONA GROUP

**612 Valley View Drive
Moline, Illinois 61265
(309) 797-8367
www.sedonagroup.com**

who walks through its doors and each client relationship. With national headquarters in Moline, Ill., The Sedona Group is the largest staffing service in the Quad-Cities. From its birth in 1986 as TemPro, a small light-industrial staffing service, it has burgeoned into a company of 4,000 staff employees and associates in more than 30 offices nationwide.

Breeding success through rock-solid solutions is a philosophy reflected in the company brand. Sedona derived its name and branding image from the awe-inspiring Cathedral Rock in Sedona, Ariz.

With people as its product, Sedona commits itself to building a force of temporary workers – called associates – who effectively and efficiently accommodate the changing needs of the companies they serve.

Best Service, People, Solutions

You could say Sedona has an extreme vision of customer service and people potential. It equips its associates with marketable skills and good work ethics at its state-of-the-art training facility. With that, associates develop a strong desire to succeed by accomplishing the changing work needs of companies large and small. The formula results in a triple-win situation:

• Clients remain more competitive by hiring the best people only when they need them;

• Providing creative, proactive staffing solutions reinforces Sedona's growing reputation;

• Associates gain the ability to build bright futures. In fact, 70 percent of Sedona associates become full-time employees at the businesses they serve.

A deep-rooted desire to see the Quad-Cities grow as a great place to live and work brought the John family into the business of helping people achieve what they want to achieve.

Rick John, president, brothers Larry and Tim, vice presidents, and father Richard, community ambassador, lead the team that broadens the value of every person who seeks their assistance in finding employment.

Extensive, free-of-charge training and placement opportunities allow associates to unlock their unlimited potential. It's an appealing proposition that attracts an average of 700 new faces to Sedona each month.

Total Workforce Management

Sedona services are extensive. The core of the business staffs office support, light industrial, technical, engineering and nursing positions.

Through its comprehensive technologies division, Sedona offers computer programming and consulting; direct and contract information technology hires; data consulting and management; corporate staff training services.

It has achieved ISO 9001 certification, an international standard that requires implementation and maintenance of quality management systems that ensure customer satisfaction.

The Johns take their mission of shaping futures a step further into the Quad-Cities' community through enthusiastic involvement on a civic level.

By placing their energies and talents to work in the community, and encouraging others to do the same, they believe the Quad-Cities can continue to develop as a vibrant place to live, work and succeed.

Those efforts were rewarded in 2003 when President Rick John was inducted into the Junior Achievement Quad-Cities Area Business Hall of Fame, which recognizes outstanding local business leaders who have succeeded in the free-market economy and moved our society in a better, stronger direction.

At left, staff employees at the Sedona headquarters in Moline direct the broad spectrum of services that provide cutting-edge total workforce management solutions for hundreds of companies nationwide. Led by the John family, front, from left, Larry, Tim, Richard and Rick, the company continues its growth of new offices and new markets. Above, the company brand exemplifies Sedona's philosophy for rock-solid solutions. Below, Sedona's Moline learning center provides unlimited scholarship training to build the skills of Sedona associates.

RELAX TO THE SOUNDS OF A SOOTHING PIANO AS YOU LOUNGE IN THE SPACIOUS AND WELL-APPOINTED LOBBY. DELIGHT IN THE EXPANSIVE FLORAL AND FAUNA SURROUNDING THE LOVELY LAGOON. A FRIENDLY, DEDICATED STAFF AND THE BEST CARE AWAIT YOU.

Above, Trinity's 7th Street Campus in Moline, Ill., continues to expand home-like services. In the spring of 2004, the campus will open its $10 million obstetrical unit. Below, Trinity at Terrace Park opens in February 2004. This $72 million, 150-bed, full-service hospital in Bettendorf, Iowa, is filled with advanced technology and also gardens, waters and prairie pathways that promote wellness for all who use them.

It all may sound like the vacation spa and resort of your dreams. But, in fact, this is the everyday working world of Trinity Regional Health System. With a passion for patient comfort and satisfaction, Trinity takes unprecedented approaches to provide the finest that health care can offer.

Trinity's three hospitals – the West Campus in Rock Island, Ill.; the 7th Street Campus in Moline, Ill.; and Trinity at Terrace Park, scheduled to open in Bettendorf, Iowa, in February 2004 – are the nuclei of the regional health system's new brand of health care.

A New Brand of Care

Trinity Regional Health System, with Quad-City roots dating back to 1893, was created in 1992 with the merger of Moline's United Medical Center and Rock Island's Franciscan Medical Center. Not long after the merger, Trinity leaders took a strategic stance to embrace an emerging philosophy that focused on a residential-like culture that would emotionally, physically and spiritually provide a more positive health-care experience, not just for patients, but also for their families, visitors, staff and volunteers.

This new brand of Trinity care began in 1997 with the construction of the 7th Street Campus, an upscale, home-away-from-home hospital facility. Warm colors, panoramic views, beautiful land-scaping and friendly décor proved to help divert the host of issues that emotionally drain someone who is sick. In both theory and reality, the setting delivers a feeling of well being and expert care.

Trinity since has duplicated the stunning architectural style and design elements at its new Bettendorf campus. The West Campus, too, is taking on the aesthetically pleasing characteristics of its younger siblings through ongoing renovation projects that are upgrading the atmosphere of Trinity's largest facility.

Delivering Care and Compassion

Moving away from a non-institutional environment meant more than changing aesthetics. Trinity's best-of-class reputation has much to do with the distinctiveness of the Trinity team, which President and Chief Executive Officer Bill Leaver describes as "the very core of Trinity's success." Its dedicated board of trustees is devoted to fulfilling the Trinity mission; loyal employees and volunteers take pride in Trinity's focus on best practices and continual improvement; and the physicians on staff utilize their superb skill and knowledge, combined with the finest technology and facilities, to achieve desired medical results. With more than 2,700 employees, Trinity is one of the largest employers in the region.

Patient satisfaction is more than a baseless marketing mantra at Trinity. Extensive staff training ensures that behavioral standards

Oregionality

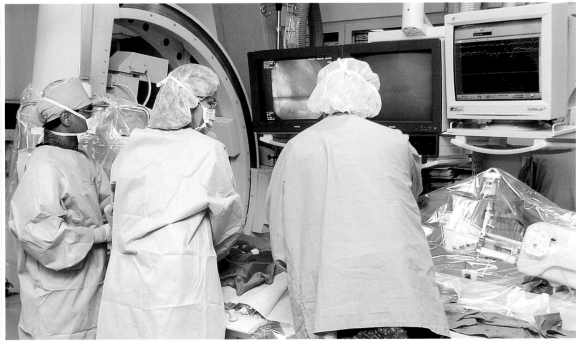

At left, combining state-of-the-art technology with the human touch, Trinity's Heart Center provides personalized care through a broad spectrum of services that help patients return to full and vibrant lives. Below left, the new campus of the Trinity College of Nursing and Health Sciences is testimony to Trinity's commitment to addressing the nation's nursing shortage. Founded in 1898, the college enjoys a rich heritage in preparing health-care professionals for the workforce. Below right, through caring, compassion and creativity, nurses of the Trinity-affiliated Visiting Nurse and Homemaker Association provide transitional health services that help patients manage diseases, achieve recovery goals and regain independence.

help achieve medical goals. From telephone and elevator etiquette to patient sensitivity and healing, the Trinity team recognizes the benefits of treating each person individually based on needs, resources and lifestyle.

This patient-centered care is an integral, unifying theme in Trinity's mission, values and philosophy. At Trinity, achieving inpatient, outpatient and recovery goals require four essential components:

• Honoring and respecting individual patient needs and rights
• Emphasizing access to information and education
• Encouraging family involvement in patient care
• Making special efforts to create an environment – and all the aspects of care – comfortable and non-intimidating.

Hospital management supports staff by efficiently and effectively addressing needs and recognizing employees for jobs well done. This can-do, above-and-beyond management style is evident throughout Trinity, and includes new on-site employee child-care facilities at both the West Campus and at Terrace Park. Attention to staff needs and great communication translate into employees who embrace the Trinity philosophy for customer care and satisfaction.

Volunteers also are an important component of the Trinity team. More than 1,000 strong, teens and adults bring community embodiment into the organization, taking on tasks that help Trinity staff operate more efficiently and effectively. In addition, the Trinity Auxiliary focuses on philanthropic endeavors that benefit patients, visitors, employees and communities, and Befrienders serve to build the confidence of

At right, Trinity maternity services combine the old-fashioned comforts of home with the best in modern technology. An attentive and highly skilled staff, a warm supportive setting and a family-centered program make this important moment as special as possible. Below, Trinity's Cancer Center has a proven record of accomplishment in cancer research, helping patients obtain access to the newest clinical trials.

Trinity Key Services

Bariatric Surgery
  (surgical weight loss)
Diabetes Center
Illinois Resource Hospital
Level II Neonatal Intensive Care
  Nursery
Level II Trauma Center
Maternity Center
Pain Clinic
Robert Young Center for
  Community Mental Health
Sleep Lab
Trinity Cancer Center
Trinity Clinics
Trinity Diagnostic Center
Trinity Enrichment Center
Trinity Express Care
Trinity Health Enterprises
Trinity Health Foundation
Trinity Heart Center
Trinity Home Care Products
Trinity Physician Hospital
  Organization (PHO)
Trinity Rehabilitation Services
Trinity Women's Health Clinics
Wound Care

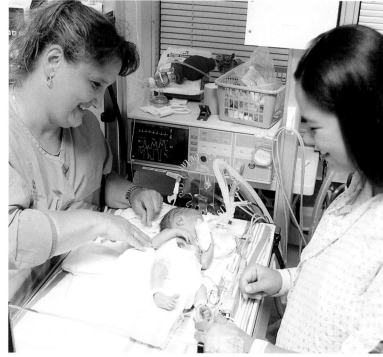

patients and their families through loving care.

The charitable arm of Trinity, the Trinity Health Foundation, is a nonprofit, philanthropic organization that annually awards more than $200,000 in grants and scholarships that promote the healthy well being of the Quad-City area. Proud and humbled to be chosen as the vehicle that expresses the social commitments of public and private donors, the foundation board of 20 local community leaders and staff conscientiously focus on funding causes that support needed health-related programs and services of Trinity and the broader communi-

ty. For example, grants include funding for medication and supplies for the working poor; a church-based parish nurse program that delivers preventive and educational services to more than 50 area congregations; nursing scholarships; high-tech medical equipment and community health outreach services.

Quality Care, Always

You can assume – and you would be correct – that Trinity offers comprehensive, top-quality health care across the board. Trinity Regional Health System is a senior affiliate of Iowa Health System, the largest integrated health system in Iowa. This partnership delivers many advantages. Most impressively, hundreds of the health system's primary physicians share knowledge, research and experience to solve challenges, thereby delivering health-care benefits of the highest possible quality and lowest possible cost.

Trinity goes to great lengths to measure and improve quality and satisfaction standards, continually raising the bar by surveying and analyzing the care of every person served at its facilities. Trinity man-

agement sets priorities for improvements based on this customer input. From conveniences, such as computerized bedside registration and charting, to personalized rehabilitation, such as Trinity's cardiac rehab program, any service that can improve the wellness of patients and garner positive results is considered for implementation.

Trinity takes satisfaction to an extreme, with senior leaders personally handling patient concerns. Physicians, too, stay informed through patient satisfaction surveys. Trinity's attention to quality, satisfaction, superior facilities, ethics and technologies are why hundreds of top-quality primary care and specialty physicians choose to be affiliated with Trinity.

Trinity's progressive approaches and partnerships deliver impressive results. For example, concerning patient satisfaction, Trinity emergency-room care ranks in the 99th percentile within a peer group of several hundred hospitals, and overall patient approval ratings exceed the 90th percentile. Often recognized for its quality, Trinity even received the coveted Ernest A. Codman National Award for effective use of performance measurement to improve the quality of patient care. It won an unprecedented second Codman Award through the Iowa Health System for its efforts to help patients successfully manage their diabetes. The Codman Award is presented by health care's premiere authority on performance improvement -- The Joint Commission on Accreditation of Healthcare Organizations. And Trinity has been recognized further with a silver level State of Illinois Lincoln Award for Business Excellence. This award is the   state version of the prestigious Malcolm Baldridge National Quality Award.

Promoting A Well Community

Beyond treating illnesses, injuries and disease, Trinity improves the health of the community by reaching out through many initiatives, an important component of its commitment to wellness.

For example, Trinity's community health screenings, a service of the Visiting Nurse and Homemaker Association's Wellness Program, work with the under-served who may not have easy access to a physician. Through respiratory, cholesterol, blood pressure and other screenings, nurses work to educate patients on preventive measures they can take to improve overall health.

Extensive rehabilitation services expedite healing and wellness processes. Education, therapy and in-home services, such as visiting nurse and parish nurse care, deliver one-to-one assistance that help patients accept limitations, remain independent and advance their lives as viable members of society.

Another outreach program enhances quality of life. The Trinity Enrichment Center works to improve relationships, and offers non-traditional methods of doing so. It offers such seminars as "Women in Midlife Adventure," "Making Love Last" and "Mommy-To-Be Massage," among dozens of others for women, couples, fathers, mothers and friends.

Growing Through Innovation

Trinity's 15 community clinics bring convenience to customers. Clinics, including three specifically for women, serve more than 11,000 patients per month, and expand beyond city limits to better serve rural residents.

Trinity's subsidiary, the Robert Young Center for Community Mental Health, a comprehensive

mental health center that annually serves almost 6,500 individuals, is a valuable partner that melds proper mental and physical health care that is so important to improving wellness. The center's numerous inpatient and outpatient services use a strength-based approach that recognizes and focuses on individual capabilities that can improve the overall welfare of each person.

Trinity also operates several health-care businesses:
Trinity Ambulance Service;
A Physician Hospital Organization, a health-management company that provides health-benefit packages to area employers using comprehensive services available through Trinity and a select panel of physicians;
Trinity Home Care Products, which carries a full-line of medical equipment and supplies available for sale and rental in both Iowa and Illinois; Work Fitness Center, which provides expertise to area businesses through its occupational health and wellness programs.

The humanization and person-

alization that Trinity extends to patients and communities positively affect individuals and communities in countless ways. Through excellence, flexibility, integrity, responsiveness, service and teamwork, Trinity Regional Health System has proven itself to be an organization committed to learning, to being an outstanding employer, an indispensable community partner and the health-care provider of choice throughout the Mississippi River Bend Region.

Above, Trinity's most recent innovation in mental health care is the Robert Young Center Community Support Program facility, named District 22. This state-of-the-art center combines therapy with recreational opportunities, including this non-alcoholic bar, a stadium-style surround-sound theater and facilities that teach skills. Below, non-traditional recovery methods include Trinity's Pet Therapy.

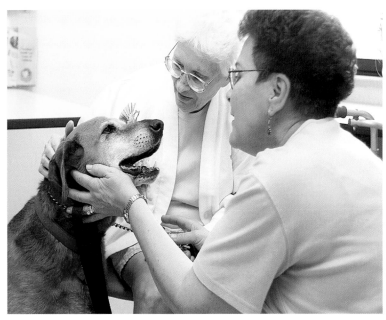

TRINITY
IOWA HEALTH SYSTEM

TRINITY REGIONAL
HEALTH SYSTEM
2701 17th St.
Rock Island, Illinois 61201
(309) 779-5000
www.trinityqc.com

U.S. Bank and Bechtel Trusts and Foundation

At right, Ken Koupal, president of the Quad-City Metro Region of US Bank, and on the left, Richard "Dick" Bittner, chairman of the board, provide strong leadership to one of the region's largest banking corporations. Below, the interior of the U.S. Bank Center in downtown Davenport recalls a more ornate time. Below bottom, the bank's clock has kept time for generations.

The 'Roaring Twenties'

Charlie Chaplin was the "Little Tramp" and Douglas Fairbanks and Mary Pickford reigned as king and queen at the box office. And the Tri-Cities, as they were known, were in the midst of economic growth and prosperity ... and local Davenport business leader, George M. Bechtel formed the Bechtel Trust Company in 1927 which became First Trust and Savings Bank in 1935, a forerunner of U.S. Bank's presence in the Quad-Cities. Through a series of mergers and acquisitions, U.S. Bank was created and Bechtel's First Trust and Savings Bank became an integral part of the largest banking corporation in the Quad-Cities.

Celebrating 150 years

Established in 1853, U.S. Bank is celebrating 150 years of serving communities. Though a long history of community involvement, employees are encouraged to take active roles in the communities they live. Through the U.S. Bancorp Foundation in 2002, the company provided more than $22 million in cash grants to a wide range of qualified nonprofit organizations. From affordable housing to art museums, from youth mentorship to United Way, U.S. Bancorp Foundation helped communities achieve their dreams in 2002. U.S. Bank is structured so every community has seasoned leaders, capable managers and an employee base committed to their local market. These leadership teams know their markets and the people in them; we know the Quad-Cities and what it takes to build a strong economic base; and we understand the businesses and industries that make the Quad-Cities' communities strong.

Every community counts

US Bank's philosophy of providing community leadership and supporting worthwhile organizations has surfaced in the Quad-Cities with contributions to such organizations as the Davenport Museum of Art with land donations and financing of the new Figge Arts Center. In addition, U.S. Bank has also been a major sponsor for the holiday tradition, Festival of Trees; the Scott County Family YMCA and Two Rivers YMCA in Moline; DavenportOne; the Bettendorf Economic Growth Corp; Renew Moline, D.A.R.I. (Downtown Association of Rock Island) and much more. Its support of the Quad City Botanical Center has been a major factor in the success of this exciting addition to downtown Rock Island. Efforts to reach other members of the community include sponsorship of the Moonlight Chase in Eldridge and Moline's Viva Quad Cities. The vision of U.S. Bank to become the best bank in America for Hispanics is being realized by committing unparalleled products, services and support to their community.

U.S. Bank is committed to providing all its members with the most convenient access for all their banking needs. Through their exclusive Five Star Service Guarantee, U.S. Bank ensures the performance standards their customers expect and deserve.

"I am very proud to be a part of this dynamic community. As a major supporter of many Quad-Cities' organizations and events, we are pleased to be able to make a difference in the lives of Quad-Citians. Our Five Star Service Guarantees ensures our dedication to excellence," said Kenneth R. Koupal, president, Quad-City Metro Region, U.S. Bank.

The Bechtel Trusts and Foundation

Harold R. Bechtel was one of Iowa's leading businessmen and bankers.

Marie H. Bechtel was highly regarded for her cultural activities and interest in the health and well being of the citizens of Scott County. She also was known for her devotion to the hospitals in her community and provided countless hours in serving these needs.

The Bechtel Foundation, an Iowa not-for-profit corporation, was formed in 1964 by Harold and Marie Bechtel. They served as trustees and founders of the four Bechtel Charitable Trusts naming R. Richard Bittner as trustee. The Trusts and Foundation were established to create investment income to be used for charitable, scientific, literary, and educational purposes. The larger trusts were primarily funded with First Trust's common stock. Those trusts today have a substantial interest in U.S. Bank's common stock.

Most of the philanthropic benefits are restricted to Scott County, Iowa. The Bechtels were born in Davenport, Iowa. Harold served in World War I and World War II. During the second world war he achieved the rank of Lieutenant Colonel. Following World War I he became engaged in the banking industry. The Bechtel Trust

Company originally organized by his father, George M. Bechtel, received its state banking charter in 1935 and became First Trust and Savings Bank. Harold served as chairman of the board. Even at age 90, Mr. Bechtel continued to be a driving force at the bank. In 1987, before his death, he continued as a key decision maker in moving the Firstar Bank Davenport, N.A. (formally First Bank and Trust and Savings Bank) from its original location at 3rd and Brady streets to its (U.S. Bank) present location at 2nd and Main streets in Davenport. Mr. Bechtel was very proud of the fact that he was able to create employment for members of his community. Mr. Bechtel was respected for his strong civic and business leadership, serving on the board of directors of many local businesses and organizations.

"I have lived the entirety of my long and rewarding life in, about and as a resident of Scott County. I have engendered a great love of the community, its institutions, and the surroundings ... that it is the youth of the community who, in many instances, provide the stimulation, energy, and motivation for perpetuation of many of the good things," said Mr. Bechtel.

The Bechtel Trusts and Foundation have given gifts of $25 million since its charitable inception in 1987. The Bechtel

Trusts and Foundation's value in 1987 was $18 million. The Bechtel Trusts and Foundation have provided many opportunities and have helped build the cultural spirit in and around the Quad-Cities.

The Bechtel Trusts and Foundation have supported many projects and helped them come to a successful conclusion. Here are just a few of them: $15 million to Revitalization of Downtown Davenport; $4 million to the City of Davenport; $1 million to formation of the Adler Foundation; $1 million to The Figge Arts Center; $600,000 to The Kahl Building Renovation; $400,000 to The Quad-City Sports Center; $400,000 to DavenportOne Foundation; $400,000 to Quad-City Botanical Center, Rock Island; $300,000 to Junior Achievement Exchange City; $250,000 to Downtown Davenport Public Library and many more.

During their lifetimes, Marie H. and Harold R. Bechtel took great pride in Harold's ability of utilizing capital in a manner that provided meaningful employment and a strong community. The legacy of the Bechtel Trusts and Foundation will live forever in our community.

For a Grant application form contact: Luci Oseland, 1000 U.S. Bank Center, 201 West Second Street, Davenport, Iowa 52801.

The Bechtel Trusts and Foundation has helped fund several high-profile project, including the Quad-City Sports Center (top left), new downtown public parking facilities (top right) and the JA Exchange City building (above).

U.S. BANK, N.A.

US Bank Center
201 West Second Street
Davenport, Iowa 52801
563-328-3100
www.usbank.com

THE BECHTEL TRUSTS AND FOUNDATION

1000 US Bank Center
201 West Second Street
Davenport, Iowa 52801

O VER THE PAST 30 YEARS, GENEROUS CONTRIBUTIONS TOTALING MORE THAN $160 MILLION HAVE ALLOWED UNITED WAY OF THE QUAD CITIES AREA TO INVEST IN PROGRAMS AND INITIATIVES THAT BENEFIT PEOPLE RIGHT HERE IN OUR LOCAL COMMUNITY.

UNITED WAY OF THE QUAD CITIES AREA

**3247 East 35th Street Court
Davenport, Iowa 52807
Office (563) 355-4310
InfoLINK (563) 359-9900
www.unitedwayqc.org**

Above, children show how much they appreciate their counselor during a United Way-funded after-school program. At right, volunteers participate in the United Way Day of Caring. Below, United Way volunteers and staff position themselves at busy Quad-City intersections to say thanks to community residents for their generous support of United Way.

United Way contributors come from every sector of the Quad-Cities area. As one United Way, it achieves success by bringing partners together to address issues that matter most.

A Focus on What Matters

With a mission to improve lives and make a positive impact in our community by mobilizing people and resources, the United Way achieves incredible results. The United Way Community Impact Fund focuses on helping people and our community thrive. For example:

- *Successful Children and Youth:* This focus ensures children and youth have access to affordable, quality care and education. United Way invests in programs that help provide opportunities for children to grow and achieve their full potential and keep children involved in community service and leadership activities. Children and youth enjoy healthy, social, emotional, cognitive and physical development.
- *Strong Families:* This focus helps provides access to affordable quality services and support for families, ensuring they live in safe and healthy environments. In turn, families trust, respect and cooperate with each other and have access to support, networking and education for parents.

- *Healthy, Self-Reliant People:* Funds assist those in need with access to mental, emotional, physical health and terminal illness services, allowing them to lead full lives by overcoming disabilities or maintaining an active senior lifestyle. They also have access to job training, work experience and transitional services that foster long-term independence.
- *A Caring Community:* This community-support component gives families and individuals access to shelter, food and support during times of disaster or crisis. It helps neighbors look out for one another and provides places to get answers when they need help. Citizens participate and create positive impacts.

Commitment and Dedication

Nothing significant happens without the strong commitment of many dedicated people. United Ways' many successes as a community organization comes thanks to thousands of generous contributors, dedicated volunteers and partners who make the Quad-Cities a great place to live, work and grow. The time, talents and commitment of the United Way of the Quad Cities Area volunteers help maintain low overhead and truly serve the community. The United Way thanks the hundreds of community volunteers who dedicate themselves to annual fundraising, allocation research, marketing, training and so much more.

Oregionality

YOU'LL NEVER SEE A SAD PERSON EATING A WHITEY'S ICE CREAM CONE. THAT'S BECAUSE IT'S A REAL SCOOP OF HAPPINESS AND A RARE JEWEL IN THE WORLD OF ICE CREAM. AND ALTHOUGH OWNERS JON AND JEFF TUNBERG CAN DROP NAMES OF FAMOUS CUSTOMERS ALL DAY LONG, THE HEART

WHITEY'S ICE CREAM

**2525 41st Street
Moline, Illinois 61265
(309) 762-2175
(888) 5WHITEY
www.whiteysicecream.com**

of Whitey's belongs to Quad-Citians. The Tunberg family has been a part of Whitey's since 1935. Just two years after Chester "Whitey" Lindgren opened the little ice cream shop in Moline, Ill., Whitey hired 15-year-old Bob Tunberg – Jon and Jeff's dad – to help out. In 1953, Bob and his wife, Norma, "scooped" up a purchase offer from Bob's mentor and friend, and the rest is history with a delicious twist.

The Tradition Continues

Jon and Jeff grew up working with and observing their father and realized the value of great customer service and hard work. The reputation and popularity of their dad's corner store helped grow the company through the years to nine Quad-City locations. Now the "boys" work side-by-side as the company's vice presidents. The title of president remains open in honor of their father, the Quad-Cities' favorite ice cream man, who passed away in 1991.

Today, Whitey's Ice Cream continues to flourish. Nine familiar, ultra-clean, red-and-white-striped stores cheerfully beckon fans in the Iowa and Illinois Quad-Cities, and two have proven their extended appeal in Iowa City and Coralville, Iowa.

Moreover, the company door is now open to the whole country through online ordering that whisks the frozen delights via FedEx to Whitey's ice-cream-craving customers. It also distributes its product to grocery stores in a 100 mile radius.

Sweet Success

So, what is it that makes Whitey's ice cream superi-

or? The Tunbergs credit a quality product, of course, but also the shops' clean environment, fair prices and a knowledgeable, friendly staff. Whitey's all adds up to a great experience from the moment a customer enters the parking lot until that last finger-licking bite.

Oh! About those famous people and places that delight in Whitey's ice cream. Neil Diamond, The White House, Rodney Dangerfield, Garth Brooks and Payne Stewart … well, you get the picture. They, like all Quad-Citians, truly appreciate the finer things of life. That's why, when ice cream comes to mind, people come to Whitey's.

Above, owners Jon, left, and Jeff Tunberg exhibit what makes people smile when they visit Whitey's Ice Cream. Center, Moline's 41st Street location is indicative of the inviting charm of Whitey's 11 locations. Below, original owner Chester "Whitey" Lindgren, left, and Bob Tunberg, who bought the business in 1953, demonstrate the trademark feature of a Whitey's shake.

Wﬁ A MISSION TO PASSIONATELY DELIVER INNOVATIVE FINANCIAL SOLUTIONS, WELLS FARGO BANK ENABLES CUSTOMERS TO FULFILL THEIR DREAMS. PERSONALIZED CUSTOMER SERVICE AND COMMUNITY INVOLVEMENT ARE HALLMARKS OF THIS PREMIER FINANCIAL SERVICES COMPANY.

At top right, Wells Fargo Cash Vault Department employees have combined service of more than 300 years. Members of the Wells Fargo Bank Quad-Cities Management Team (pictured at right) are, Darryl Harmon, senior vice president, Commercial Division Manager; Scott Asher, vice president, Community Banking Manager; John Stavnes, president Eastern Iowa; and Sandra Fording, assistant vice president, Public Relations Manager Eastern Iowa. Below, Wells Fargo employees and their families participate in the 2003 Old Fashioned Fourth of July Parade in Bettendorf.

While Wells Fargo has a reputation as one of America's most outstanding companies, it is the history of its Davenport location and talented employees – many of whom served predecessor banks Davenport Bank and Trust, Bettendorf Bank and Trust and Brenton Bank – that enable Wells Fargo to carry on local traditions of delivering superb customer service and valued community support.

History – 151 Years Strong

Founded in 1852, Wells Fargo established its first office in Iowa in 1872. Operating 77 banking stores in more than 45 Iowa communities, the Wells Fargo family employs 9,700 employees in its Iowa Mortgage, Financial and Banking divisions.

Locally, in Davenport, Wells Fargo is home to regional headquarters for eastern Iowa and western Illinois, with 400 team members.

Today, Wells Fargo Bank is the state's top SBA, agricultural, small business, mortgage and home-equity lender and is a leader in Internet banking with four million online users nationwide. As Iowa's largest financial institution, Wells Fargo ranks first statewide in deposit market share with $6.5

billion in deposits.

Wells Fargo Bank is a steadfast partner in the community. Loans for homes and home improvements, businesses, autos, education and lines of credit daily enrich the lives of citizens throughout the region. At its locations on both sides of the Mississippi River, employees take great pride in knowing their customers on a first-name basis while,

at the same time, bringing the advantages of its world-wide financial resources to "Main Street U.S.A." banking.

John Stavnes, president of Wells Fargo Eastern Iowa, strongly believes that what makes a bank local is how it serves its community. The local Wells Fargo banking family enjoys pulling together to give back to communities its time, talent and treasures.

Sharing Time and Talent

According to John Stavnes, president of Wells Fargo Eastern Iowa, "When a bank prospers, the community prospers, and positive results are the outcome." To achieve its goal of helping make the region a better place to live, work and play, bank employees have contributed more than 115,000 hours of time and talents to community organizations over the past 10 years.

"We are a community bank. I can say that unequivocally because a community bank is defined by how well customers are treated, their level of community support and involvement and where and how banking decisions are made... we are the Quad-Cities 'hometown' bank," said Stavnes.

Employees support causes ranging from scout groups to churches to schools. More than 48,000 of these hours supported Wells Fargo corporate sponsorships, including: American Heart Association Heart Walk; American Diabetes Association Walk; Festival of Trees; Gilda's Club Week of Laughter; March of Dimes Walk America; Mississippi Valley Fair; Race for the Cure; Rebuilding Together; Quad City Symphony Riverfront Pops Concert.

Your Sucess Is Our Sucess

Wells Fargo also is committed to sharing the knowledge of its leaders with area organizations. Some 57 bank officers are involved as board members, officers and key committee members

with more that 100 civic, cultural, educational and social service groups. Among these are: Bettendorf Chamber of Commerce; Boys and Girls Club; Davenport Schools Foundation; DavenportOne; Family Resources; Gilda's Club; Habitat for Humanity; and many more.

In addition, Wells Fargo feels strongly about supporting local charities and community development through cash donations. Over the past 10 years, more than $4.5 million has infused new life into various initiatives, including: Bettendorf Fund; Birdies for Charity; Blackhawk College Foundation; Boy Scouts of America; Boys and Girls Club; Center for Aging Services; Community Health Care; DavenportOne; Development Association of Rock Island; Family Museum of Arts and Science; Family Resources; Gilda's Club; Habitat of Humanity; Mississippi Valley Regional Blood Center; Mississippi Valley Neighborhood Housing Services; Putnam Museum/IMAX® Theatre and more.

Top left, Wells Fargo is a major corporate sponsor of the Quad City Symphony Riverfront Pops concert in Davenport's LeClaire Park. Above, one of the largest summer gatherings in the Quad Cities is the Wells Fargo Street Festival, which benefits DavenportOne Downtown Partnership. The event is held during Bix Weekend in Downtown Davenport. Sponsored by the bank, the fair's array of food, arts, crafts, music and children's activities annually attracts thousands of people. Below, Wells Fargo employee volunteers serve beverages during the popular street fest.

WELLS FARGO BANK

203 West Third Street
Davenport, Iowa 52801
(563) 383-3211
www.wellsfargo.com

Photographers

While they come from all walks of life, our 100-plus Oregionality photographers all have two things in common — a passion for photography and a fondness of all the wonderful assets of life in eastern Iowa and western Illinois — our Mississippi River Bend region. Here is just a small sampling of our amateur and professional contributors, including the photography staff at the Quad-City Times, our top five Oregionality photo contest winners and other artistic residents who helped make this book possible.

Dorole D. King

Karla A. Pinner

Sharon Beckman

GREG BOLL has had his photographs published in *The New York Times, Los Angeles Times, London Daily Mail* and *Forbes* magazine, as well as many other national and regional publications. The *Quad-City Times* photojournalist became interested in photography at an early age. "I grew up around photography; my father was a combat photographer in WWII and then worked as a newspaper photographer for almost 50 years. I learned at an early age all of the free access to events a news photographer had," Boll says. His father was a big influence on his career. "I can't remember when I first picked up a camera, but I still remember walking the sidelines of Iowa football games with my dad and using an old Nikon F with motordrive and a 135 mm lens," he says. Using a telephoto lens at its widest aperture to blow out backgrounds for a clean, graphic effect is one his favorite techniques. His favorite camera equipment is the Canon EOS1N for film and Canon Digital cameras.

JEFF COOK, a *Quad-City Times* photojournalist, became interested in photography in the second grade. "My dad had a German Kodak Retina camera, and we watched slides on the living room wall," he said. He graduated from the University of Iowa's school of journalism. His photographs have appeared in several publications. "During a

period of record cold winter temperatures, I took a photo of a Clinton, Iowa, man with icicles hanging from his mustache – this covered two pages in *Parade* magazine," he said.

LARRY FISHER is a staff photographer for the *Quad-City Times*. He says his favorite photo subjects are those he takes for spot news. Fisher has had his photography published in *Newsweek, Time* and the *St. Petersburg (Fla.) Times*, among many other national and regional newspapers. In addition, he has contributed photographs to numerous books. He has a bachelor of fine arts from Kansas City Art Institute.

LEIGH ANN NIXON always wanted to be a photographer and says one of her goals is to always be able to enjoy taking pictures. She is the advertising photographer at the *Quad-City Times* and an ad designer. "I really got interested in photography because my dad enjoys photography as a hobby. I learned from him, took classes and learned through my job – experience is a great teacher," she said. Photography fits well into other aspects of her life as well. "My husband, Andy, our dog, Jimmy, and I all go out on our boat, either on the Mississippi or a lake in Wisconsin ... Andy fishes, Jimmy barks, and I take photos." Leigh Ann has had her photos published in the *International Library of*

Photography 2002 Anthology Palette of Dreams, the *Bettendorf News* and the *Quad-City Times*.

JOHN SCHULTZ is a graduate of the University of Iowa's school of journalism and is a *Quad-City Times* photojournalist. "I've always wanted to know what's going on – so I got into journalism. … I like to watch people and study their weird habits. It takes patience and persistence to capture that right moment." In addition, Schultz appreciates the technological advances the digital age has produced. "Digitals have been a wonderful advancement in the field." He has had his photography published in *Sports Illustrated, Newsweek, Country Woman*, the *Los Angeles Times, Runner's World* and the *Chicago Tribune*.

KEVIN ALLCHIN of Davenport says a photography assignment years ago inspired him to keep taking photographs as an art form and hobby. "While I was in high school, I took a picture of my sister-in-law's eye. I super-imposed the photo of the eye onto a photo of an egg sitting on a table. That earned me an A in photography class. Since then I have traveled to many countries, and I enjoy capturing their different cultures on film." Allchin says he intends to keep doing photography as a hobby and art form. Taking photographs fits in

Oregionality

Karen Gilmore

Jo Ann Whitmore

well with his other interests. "I enjoy photographing my two boys, ages 7 and 8. And they have already started to take their own pictures ... but we have ended up with 20 copies of our hamster." Allchin's photographs have been published in the *Quad-City Times*, the *Rock Island Argus*, the *Moline Dispatch* and the *Muscatine Journal*. Using a Nikon F-3, Allchin says he makes many of his own filters to achieve the right effects.

BOB CAWLEY of Rock Island began his photography career with a casual interest, but over the years it has grown into a hobby. Cawley says one of his goals while shooting a photograph is to "freeze time, so the scene can be visited and enjoyed many times over." Photography is the perfect vehicle for Cawley, who enjoys taking his camera on the road. Until *Oregionality*, Cawley only had published his photos on the Internet. "I like shooting several things, but I like taking pictures of sunsets and ducks flying by," he says.

PHILIP CUNNINGHAM of Moline says he's proud of his amateur photographer's status once again. A graduate of Western Illinois University, Macomb, Cunningham worked many years as a professional photojournalist for the *Quad-City Times and Rock Island Argus*. He also has done work for many national publications. Cunningham says he always cherished his friendships and the camaraderie between his fellow photographers and newsmen. "Not a day goes by I don't take my camera when I'm traveling. I love to capture life's small moments and to share these with my family, co-workers and friends," he says. He works mostly with his Nikon D100 digital camera in conjunction with Adobe Photoshop.

SHIRLEY DICKEY of Eldridge, Iowa, especially looks for things to photograph that others might normally ignore. "Some of my favorite subjects to shoot are landscapes, cloud formations, nature and things that have historical significance. I've used a camera since, I was old enough to have one and buy the film." As an artist, photography fits well into the retired schoolteacher's life. "I use photos to draw and paint from ... for my own personal fun," she says.

JACK GREER of Davenport likes still-life and scenic subjects. Greer became involved in photography when he was younger. "I used to look at other's pictures and was sure I could do it as good or better. I've always enjoyed scenery and all the colors. His photos in *Oregionality* mark his first time published. "I like to use shadows in my photographs, so I tend to take pictures in the early morning or late afternoons." When it comes to photography, Greer waxes philosophically. "Photography is like writing a book – you have to wait for the next inspiration."

MELISSA HAEGELE says her interest in photography was because of her father. "He let me use his camera, and for the past four years I've been entering my photographs in the 4-H competitions," she says. Haegele, who is a student, plans to major in graphic design in college and continue to better her photography skills. "I enjoy art and photography provides me another outlet to express my creativity. My favorite subjects to photograph are flowers, scenery and people." Her photographs in *Oregionality* are the first ones published.

TRACY HAYES of Moline has been a professional photographer since 1984. Her photographs have appeared in the *Quad-City Times, Bloomberg News, Cosmopolitan, Parade* and many others. She earned a bachelor's degree from Arizona State University in photojournalism, journalism and public relations. She has a master's degree in organizational leadership and will receive her MBA in organizational management from St. Ambrose University in December 2003. "I've been a commercial photographer for 19 years and was drawn into the medium as a component of my fine art. My lifetime goal is to be making images when I'm 80," she says.

MITZI SUE HOOK of Thomson, Ill., began taking photographs of her son and "progressed from there. I enjoy photography because I feel like a little kid seeing the world for the first time," she says. "I love taking photos of people, flowers, butterflies and unusual architecture." Her photographs have been published in *Hunter & Sport Horse* magazine and the *Clinton Herald*. Her camera is a Canon EOS A2. "I use a tripod for 99 percent of my work. My closeup shots are used with a 28-70mm lens with macro filters. When possible I like to use a polarizer."

QUINN KIRKPATRICK of Rock Island credits his father for starting him on the path to photography. "My father had a darkroom when I was growing up, so I was around the process early on," he says. His favorite subjects include, photographing children, landscapes, still life and mountain biking. "Photography is such a part of my life. Family is very important, and I feel that documenting one's life is very important." Kirkpatrick's work has been displayed at The Illinois Artisans gallery at Rens Lake College and the sales gallery at Quad-City Fine Arts and published in the Midwestern edition of *Bike & Brew*. "I shoot almost exclusively black and white these days, mostly with a Canon EOS and 35 mm. I recently bought an old 4x5 press camera to play around with."

Cynthia D. Doering

MARY LUCAS of Davenport says encouragement from an instructor helped further her desire to become a photographer. "I took a photography class through the adult education program and our instructor, R.M. Chappel, gave me the encouragement and praise I needed to continue with this hobby." She enjoys taking pictures of her family. "I have a very big family, and I really enjoy photographing them, especially the children."

KAREN S. MONAHAN of Low Moor, Iowa, says her love of the outdoors and wildlife also lends itself to her goal of becoming a professional wildlife photographer. "I enjoy being out in the quietness and beauty of nature." Monahan credits her father with her interest in photography. "My father bought me my first camera when I was 5 years old ... and I've never stopped shooting," she says. "I learned to develop and print 35 mm black-and-white photos at the community college two years ago, and I built a darkroom in our home. Now, I use a Canon digital SLR D60 and I like macrophotography."

JANET ROSSMILLER-MILLER of LeClaire, Iowa, says she was exposed to photography at an early age, and her inspiration came from watching her father and grandfather. "They basically took family photos and vacation photos — but very creative for that time. They made it look easy." She appreciates the mobility that photography offers and says she takes her camera with her when traveling. Her photographs have been published in the former Marycrest International University newspaper, *College Student Photography Nikon 1997* and *Canon 1998* books and displayed at a photography show at Marycrest.

SHELLEY SCHIPPER of Low Moor, Iowa, says black-and-white images often show a side of life that color doesn't capture. "I'd always been drawn to black-and-white photography as an artistic expression that is sometimes truer to life than color." Schipper says her favorite subject to photograph is nature scenes. "I love trying to capture those moments of magic that we often are too busy to notice in our day-to-day lives." She finds most of her photographic equipment on eBay, including her first 35mm camera: an old Pentax.

ROY F. SHAFT JR. of Bettendorf has been interested in photography since he was about 9 or 10 years old. He says his favorite subjects to photograph include horses and nature. "I've always been fascinated with and enjoyed the process of taking pictures." Shaft says his favorite photo format is black and white. He also develops his own film and prints, and his gear includes a Minolta 650si with a Tamron 28-300mm lens.

WILLIAM TAYLOR of Moline is a self-taught photographer. Over the past 20 years, he has captured a wide variety of nature, wildlife, scenic and architectural images from throughout the United States and parts of Canada. "My favorite geographic locations to photograph are New York, Chicago, Denver, Colorado Springs, Detroit, Utah and Midwestern farm scenes." His work has been displayed at a Quad-City gallery and as stock photography on websites, front covers of telephone directories, billboards and other advertisements, annual reports, magazines and pamphlets. He says the cameras he most frequently uses are various Nikons, Pentax, Ricoh and medium-format Mamiya.

DAN WALLACE of Davenport, who took this book's cover photograph, likes to photograph architecture, nature, portraits and transportation. "I have a design background and always enjoyed being creative at anything I do. My wife 'planted the seed' for my photography skills by giving me a camera for my birthday." *Oregionality* is the first place Wallace's pictures have been published. He has a bachelor's degree in graphic design from the former Marycrest University.

ERIC A. WEBER of Preston, Iowa, likes to photograph scenes from nature. "I try to replicate the work of Mother Nature. Capturing a particular moment in time, where the world just seems to stop." Weber says he uses digital photography as part of his job as a Web development coordinator. "I enjoy the convenience of shooting digital photography and knowing that you've captured the shot just right. You may never have a second chance to get that perfect shot." (Photo not available).

STEPHANIE WILLCOX of Moline says her 2-year-old son is her favorite subject to photograph, but she also appreciates taking pictures of the bald eagles that make the Quad-Cities their winter home. "I got my first camera two years ago when our son was born." The photographs that appear in this book came early in her experience. "The ones that were chosen were pictures I had taken with my $200 Minolta, before I took my classes and before I became a professional," she says.

ED WILSON of Bettendorf likes taking photographs of most anything, but he has his favorites. "My favorites would have to be people, flowers, wildlife and landscapes. When I am taking or looking at photographs it's like the world has stopped for a second." When he was younger, Wilson purchased his first camera, a 35 mm Minolta by delivering newspapers. "My photos and art have been used on various websites and by several companies for their advertising campaigns."

MATTHEW WINCE of Davenport says shooting landscapes and panoramas are among his favorite subjects. "Photography makes me aware of how beautiful thing can be if you look at them from the right angle." Wince has had his photographs appear in catalogs, magazines, posters and store displays. "My interest in photography began in seventh grade when my science teacher had me make a pin-hole camera."

JULES IRISH
PRINCIPAL WRITER

Oregionality writer Jules Irish is a native Quad-Citian who has been involved in area writing and public relations projects for 24 years. Her career has taken her from cub newspaper reporter to features writer and editor for an international trade magazine. Jules' public relations experience includes many years at the headquarters of Modern Woodmen of America, where she also served as senior writer. In 1995, Jules fulfilled a long-time dream to become a freelance writer and has been writing corporate communications since that time for many Quad-City organizations. She has collaborated with the *Quad-City Times* on numerous writing assignments for specialty publications. Known for her strong abilities to grasp and interpret information to meet clients' needs, Jules' deeply rooted passion for and commitment to everything that is the Quad-Cities make her a great advocate of the community and an inspired writer of *Oregionality.*

OREGIONALITY PROJECT TEAM

Front row (pictured from left to right): Doreen Williams, Terry Wilson, Jules Irish, Peggy Dykes, Janet Hill, Jeanne Ketelaar and Tom Heidgerken. Back row: Kristin Keith, Anne Kuraitis, Kristyn Verstraete, Jay Crump, Debbie McAllister, Leigh Ann Nixon and Eric Tucker. Not pictured: John Stader and Jana DeBrower.

Ben Villareal

Ed Wilson

Index of Photographers

Roy F. Shaft Jr.

Index of Profiles

Karen Monahan

*region**ality***